MW00577744

My Time to Stand

My Time to Stand

Also by Gypsy-Rose Blanchard, Melissa Moore,
and Michele Matrisciani:

Released: Conversations on the Eve of Freedom

Also by Melissa Moore:

Shattered Silence: The Untold Story of a Serial Killer's Daughter

*WHOLE: How I Filled the Fragments of My Life with
Forgiveness, Hope, Strength, and Creativity*

Also by Michele Matrisciani:

*WHOLE: How I Filled the Fragments of My Life with
Forgiveness, Hope, Strength, and Creativity*

My Time to Stand

A Memoir

Gypsy-Rose Blanchard

Melissa Moore and Michele Matrisciani

BenBella Books, Inc.
Dallas, TX

BenBella Books, Inc.
10440 N. Central Expressway
Suite 800
Dallas, TX 75231
benbellabooks.com
Send feedback to feedback@benbellabooks.com

BenBella is a federally registered trademark.

Printed in the United States of America
10 9 8 7 6 5 4 3 2 1

Library of Congress Control Number: 2024033592
ISBN 9781637745908 (hardcover)
ISBN 9781637745915 (electronic)

Editing by Rick Chillot
Copyediting by Scott Calamar
Proofreading by Rebecca Maines and Jenny Bridges
Text design and composition by Sarah Avinger
Cover design by Sarah Avinger
Cover photo by Emily Fuselier
Printed by Lake Book Manufacturing

Special discounts for bulk sales are available. Please contact bulkorders@benbellabooks.com.

*For all those who are touched or
have been touched by Munchausen syndrome by proxy,
and for those who advocate for their well-being.*

Contents

Author's Note

Everyone considers my story to be "true crime." But this book is a work of memory—my memory—and therefore is a memoir and not an outsider's investigation of my life or crime. The feelings and emotions evoked are accurate. While some of my childhood memories have faded, these particular events remain vivid. To fill in many gaps, I've relied on other people's answers to my questions. The typical disclaimers apply. Some names and other details have been changed or omitted to protect the privacy of individuals. Any resemblance between a fictionalized name and a real person is strictly coincidental. Where there are passages containing dialogue, quotation marks are used when I'm reasonably sure that the speaker's words are close to verbatim or that the speaker's actual meaning is accurately reflected. The story I share here is true to my memory, and these memories have shaped my perceptions, many of which are also shared here. This is how it was for me, what I experienced or believe I experienced.

ONE

Ça Va

That's enough.

When Dee Dee Blanchard was twenty-four years old, she gave life to me. When I was nearly twenty-four years old, I took life from her. I firmly believed that by doing so, I was saving the life she had guarded with all her might: mine. Though she certainly saw my life as "ours," at best. *We're two sides of the same penny,* she liked to say, meaning: although two things may look very different and be diametrically opposed, they're actually inseparable, two parts of the same whole.

After being incarcerated for eight and a half years, I've been learning how to navigate life on my own . . . separately. My time served includes my combined imprisonment in three facilities.

First, Greene County Jail in Springfield, Missouri, where I spent a little over a year.

Then, for a month, I was transferred to a prison for women in Vandalia, until I was relocated to the Chillicothe Correctional Center to serve the remainder of my sentence. Given all that time, and with the help of therapy, family, friends, books, and my own writing, I have examined my life, actions, and relationships in great breadth and depth. At last, I've been given access to information, documents, records, therapy sessions. I'm like a detective noticing patterns, theorizing, having lightbulb moments, and making new connections between things that used to make no sense to me. Still, while a year has passed since my release from prison, my scars, both emotional and physical, remain. The physical scars are like track marks that mock my progress.

I'm not saying I can't heal; what I am saying is that the physical representation of my trauma just adds another dimension to the healing process. Like when I'm enjoying one of life's simplest joys (food, y'all), and I dive carefree into my first cut of steak or slurp of an oyster, but then have to pause and strategize the chew. Without salivary glands and teeth, thanks to unnecessary surgeries and medications, my past will always puncture my present.

The natural Louisiana sunlight that streams into my bedroom is far more forgiving than the harsh fluorescent lights at Chillicothe Correctional Center, where I was incarcerated for the seven years after my sentencing. I have a full-length mirror now, where I can see the whole of me. In prison, I could only see glimpses of my body in an eight-inch square mirror, never quite sure whether all my parts went together.

In the warm light, my scars are less jarring than I found them to be in the past. Or maybe time is softening the marks on my body. But sometimes it's what's *not* visible that hurts us most. For me, that's true. For all the trauma inflicted on my body since childhood, it's the scar that isn't there that always travels with me. The scar that otherwise would've been there—if I hadn't asked Nick to kill my mother.

People really want to know: What was the final straw? When was the moment when I decided it was her or me? Here you go, y'all, on page three.

One month before the murder, my mother tried to cut my throat. At least that's how I saw it.

The cause of concern, suddenly, was my voice. "It's so high-pitched; it's so squeaky," my mother complained to my ear, nose, and throat specialist. I thought my voice was distinct, like my uncommon name. Or maybe it was a family trait to be proud of. We both knew women on my mother's side of the family with similar high-pitched voices. Besides, Nick said my childlike chirp was sexy, so I didn't understand the issue, and I told my mother so. Never in front of the doctors, of course. I knew better than that. But on the way home, I went on and on like, well . . . a squeaky wheel.

"There's nothing wrong with my voice," I said with a whimper, as she pushed me in my portable wheelchair to the parking lot where our car was parked, outside the hospital in downtown Kansas City.

"You heard the doctor. That voice of yours might mean there's a problem with your larynx, and that problem could be causing your sleep apnea," she said, her word final. No matter my sassing, we were going to go ahead and meet with the pulmonologist the ENT had just recommended, though we both knew very well I didn't have sleep apnea.

In fact, by this point, the entire ruse had been up between us for a while. I was twenty-three and had tried to run away twice. I'd shot her with a BB gun. She'd chained me to the bed. I was getting older and much harder to control. The older I got, the more physical and harsher her punishments became. She stopped letting me use my custom-made Jazzy HD power wheelchair because she couldn't control it. I sensed she was becoming more erratic, more desperate.

Only now do I see how her back was against a wall. The lie of the life she had created could have gotten her thrown in jail on a list of felony charges as long as the Bayou. Her watchful eye grew keener as the possibility of me standing up or speaking out became more plausible. We had achieved an unspoken standoff: I knew she was a lying, manipulative criminal. She knew nobody would believe me. Her carting me off in search of a new surgery, I believed, was her attempt to secure control.

When the pulmonologist spoke to my mother, it was as if I wasn't in the room. "Why don't we do an exploratory surgery of her larynx," he suggested. "A simple operation of the voice box will get to the bottom of any respiratory or vocal abnormalities."

What I heard was, *Let's cut Gypsy's throat for no reason at all.*

I'd had previous surgeries on my neck, and the scars brutalized me. But there was something about this particular surgery that felt more threatening than the others. Even more so than all the other body parts that had been constantly searched, explored, against my will, without my consent. I turned to my mother: "That sounds like it hurts. I don't want it. I don't want to do it." Tears didn't form; rage did. My mother put her arm around my shoulder and pressed me close, a signal to quiet down that had been programmed long ago.

"It's simple, Baby, it's painless; it will help," she said, side-eying the doctor.

What I heard was: *I don't care what you want.*

The doctor assured me there was little risk. He kneeled down to my eye level and spoke slowly to me, like English wasn't my native language. Who could blame him? He thought I had the mind of a seven-year-old. Except my trapped adult brain suddenly felt the urgency to avoid this surgery at all costs.

I've thought a lot about my heightened reaction in this very moment. You know, the neck is considered the most vulnerable part of the human body. Of course, I didn't make this connection while sitting in the doctor's office. But I do think we are wired to defend our most vulnerable parts. The muscles and blood vessels and nerves in the neck are easily strained and damaged. The scars on my neck from previous surgeries, especially the one on my salivary glands, were so pronounced because the skin on the neck is very thin.

I hate to overdo the parallels (blame it on the therapy). But so many of the medical manipulations and interventions that I went through concerned the part of me that allows for expression and truth. She muzzled my mouth shut at nighttime, with a CPAP machine for my fake sleep apnea. It was so unpleasant to sleep that way; it felt like someone was taking a bicycle tire pump and forcing a ceaseless stream of air up my nose. She numbed my mouth with Orajel, so I'd drool and slur; she was responsible for my teeth falling out due to side effects of superfluous medications. By speaking for me and scripting my every interaction, she deprived me of finding my own voice. Now, the way I saw it, my literal voice, squeaky as it might be, could be taken from me. Her final play.

My mother and the pulmonologist scheduled the operation with the same casual enthusiasm of planning a teeth cleaning. Despite my recent awakening to the reality of my life, it was here where I truly feared the scope of her malice. This surgery was completely unnecessary. *Exploratory*, the doctor called it. While all the other surgeries also had been unnecessary, this was the first occasion where I was privy to my mother's recklessness before the damage could be done.

Was this the plan for the rest of my life? To cut me up and open, piece by piece, just because she could? She was making me play Russian roulette with scalpels instead of bullets. If it wasn't the voice box surgery, the odds seemed to be increasingly in favor of me dying on one of the operating tables.

"Mama, what if they cut me wrong and then I lose my voice and I can't talk?"

I don't think she would've minded that at all.

———————————

We ignored one another on the car ride home. I looked out the window, the world passing me by, more quickly now, hazier. She steered the wheel, radar-like, navigating us back to the darkness of our house.

When we entered the door, she went one way and I bee-lined to the blue medicine basin. Her pills weren't there. Waiting for her to cross the room, without words I rolled into the bedroom, which was suffocated with stuff. I didn't have to rummage too far to find the pill bottle somewhere beneath a mess of clothes and kid costumes, hand-me-downs from well-meaning strangers. I shook three oxycodone into my mouth and swallowed them dry, drenched in disillusion: I was just another thing she hoarded.

High and numb now, I craved the fantasy world Nick and I lived in, so I messaged him. Nick and his kink world of ghastly rules was my haven, where I could let him act out anger on me that I did not myself know how to express.

"Do you remember when you told me you'd protect me from people who want to hurt me?" I asked Nick.

"Yes, darling."

"Will you still protect me?"

"Yes," Nick answered.

"Even from my mother?"

"Yes."

TWO

Cajun

*Referring to Acadians, the French-speaking people
who migrated to South Louisiana from Nova Scotia
in the eighteenth century, and their descendants*

My mama, Clauddine "Dee Dee" Blanchard, was all about her culture. She was a 100 percent born-and-bred French Cajun from a place called Golden Meadow in the great State of Louisiana. Golden Meadow is the southernmost incorporated area of Lafourche Parish, and you can list its local residents on the front and back of a sheet of looseleaf paper. Mama loved Cajun cooking, which requires the holy trinity of ingredients: onions, bell peppers, and celery. Her birth surname was Pitre, which means "clown" in French. Some people confuse it and pronounce it "Pet-tree," as in the petri dish, on which penicillin was first discovered.

You don't need to listen too hard to notice a distinct dialect among those of Cajun descent who live in Southern Louisiana. My mother couldn't pronounce the *th* sound. So when she said, "Give me that," it sounded like, "Give me dat." In fact, she H-dropped a lot; "Shave off hair" was "shave off air." No matter how her words sounded, make no mistake, Clauddine Blanchard always knew exactly what she was saying. I think when you love to tell stories, like she did, you learn early on to choose your words and their delivery with precision, the better to ensnare the listener.

My mother's first big lie, that I know of, was when she met my dad, Rod Blanchard, in 1990. Dad was seventeen years old and already working as a trawler when he met my mom at the local bowling alley. I imagine my dad back in the day as a totally chill kid who got along with everyone, no matter what friend group he belonged to. He just wanted to have a good time, go see live bands, and didn't expect anything from anyone. Signing himself out of school early, my dad was a hard worker. Still is. At the bowling alley, my mother introduced herself to him, telling him she was twenty-one.

Like in one of those eighties movies, where some geeky freshman chases after the senior homecoming queen, Dad's boy brain thought he'd scored with an older woman, one who had her own ride—a Ford Fiesta—and could legally buy him booze and be his designated driver. He just didn't know how much of an older woman she truly was. Mama was actually twenty-three years old. The question is: *Why would a woman in her twenties want an immature boy as a boyfriend?* Knowing what I know now, I suspect she thought she could manipulate or control him in a way a man her age wouldn't allow. Or maybe her insecurity made her feel that a man her age wouldn't want her. She could've just thought Dad was hot. These things can all be true at the same time.

So, they started dating: Mama driving Dad to Biloxi to barhop, going out to see hair bands in the NOLA club scene, frequenting the local dive-bar hangout the Greenhouse. Mama was really into music. When she was younger, she used to follow bands around. She claimed she was in a relationship with Jack Russell, the lead singer of the eighties hair band Great White. I was recently told by a friend of Mama's that they were both outside a concert venue waiting for the band to come out of the tour bus. And my mother managed to get a picture taken with Jack, which she framed and hung on her bedroom wall. She told anyone who saw it that Jack had mailed the photo to her because they were in a relationship, which was completely false.

Mama also claimed she was a virgin before she met my dad. I'm not about to ask my dad his opinion on this. But I know that being a groupie and a virgin cannot be true at the same time.

According to stories I've heard, Mama had a thing for lead singers and wanted to be their girlfriend. Sometimes she sent flowers to herself and told people they were from various rock stars. With lies, she created lore. She was always telling stories. That was just Dee Dee.

Was kneading together lies to bake a tasty story a learned behavior from her childhood? There are plenty of secrets in the

Pitre family that nobody talks about. I'm positive it's like that in most families. When you have a secret as big as the one my mother kept about her own father, Claude Pitre, who could blame her?

My mother was the baby of six children. And get this, of the six, half were named after their father, Claude: Claude Jr., Claudia, and Clauddine. Narcissist much? Dee Dee, as Mama was called, had dreams of being a somebody. She often made it a point to remind me that she could've been that somebody if she hadn't given it all up to take care of me.

By the time my mother was twelve, she had gained a lot of weight. According to her, she "blew up," and she tried to wrap her middle in cellophane to sweat off the fat. I can't help but think her eating disorders coincided with her gaining womanly body fat after getting her first period.

And with trying to purge the secret of what happened when my grandfather insisted on joining her during her baths.

During her eleventh and twelfth grade years, Mama lost close to two hundred pounds. Apparently, my grandmother Emma body-shamed Mama relentlessly, calling her fat. Mama began a very unhealthy diet and soon developed anorexia and bulimia. Her high school friend told me she remembers Mama eating only rice cakes for a whole year.

Mommzie Emma, as I called her, used to say her husband Claude was a "man whore," claiming he had a wandering eye. I don't know if Emma knew what Claude was doing to Dee Dee. Back then ... who knows?

When Mama was younger, Mommzie used to keep her home from school all the time, telling her she was sick when she really wasn't. My mother told me she used to drink vinegar to make her skin snow white, so she'd be more beautiful. And I guess it worked. In her senior year, in 1986, Mama was South Lafourche High School's ROTC queen. ROTC stands for Reserve Officers' Training Corps. I never knew this track is for students who want to go to college to train to become an army officer. How Mama loved to talk about this momentous event. She made it seem that after that crowning, she had been entered into pageants all around the state, except that wasn't true. I have come to find out that she attended pageants out of the obligation of being the 1986 ROTC queen. She had not been entered in any pageants after that.

I feel sad for Mama now, for wanting me to believe that one pageant was so much more than what it was. I think it was the only time in her youth when she felt truly special—and pretty. She would tell me the same stories of her glory days over and over again. How celebrities hit on her on Bourbon Street or how musicians put her name in their songs and in the liner notes of their albums. More kneading. Was she trying to get my adoration? My attention? Was she trying to make me jealous? I heard about how skinny she got, how pretty she got, and how people applauded her when she was a beauty queen. It almost seemed like she was trying to make me feel even smaller, in my wheelchair, with no teeth, malnourished, androgynous—with no attractiveness at all, most of the time dressed as a boy. I'd think: *She used to have it all until I came along.* I put her on a pedestal. I'd see pictures and think: *Wow, that was my Mama! No wonder Claude loved her most.*

Maybe I didn't follow in Mama's footsteps as a beauty queen, but when it came to Claude, I would turn out to be his favorite just like my mom had been.

I don't know when Mama's dreams died, but by the time she met my father, she was drifting. She had tried. I remember her saying, "The rest of us kids were fuckups, so I tried to do my mom proud by joining Junior ROTC and winning a beauty pageant."

At the time twenty-three-year-old hospital worker Dee Dee approached my father in a bowling alley, she had never been in a serious relationship that I know of, had only completed two years of college, and wasn't in nursing school as she had intended. She blamed the lack of achievement on having me; but I think it's the other way around. She hadn't achieved much, so caring for a chronically sick kid became the excuse or even the justification. *See, Dee Dee isn't a fuckup like the rest of those kids; poor thing's got Gypsy.*

My grandmother Sharon, my dad's mother, worked at the public library and one day noticed a book in the return bin that had Mama's name on the checkout card in the back pocket. The title was something along the lines of *How to Get Pregnant Fast.* Concerned, Sharon called her son to warn him. If you know any seventeen-year-old boys, I don't need to tell you her warning fell on deaf ears. Instead, Dad confronted Mama, who became enraged that Sharon breached the confidentiality rules of the library. Next thing you know, Mama was trying to get Sharon fired.

I know Mama had a taste for vengeance because I often witnessed it, so it makes sense that she jumped to such a vindictive act. You'd think she would've cared about the risk that her boyfriend's mother could end up hating her. Characteristically, my mother got very defensive and felt slighted by the smallest actions, even if they weren't done on purpose. She'd read into things, make assumptions about what people were thinking, take unrelated actions as personal affronts, and would shut them down in any way she could. Mama also ran away from situations and conflict a lot. Later in my life, I think she graduated from defensive to paranoid. This made it very difficult for her to have relationships, especially with her siblings. Her paranoia was partly why she isolated us from the world.

Long story short, the pregnancy book worked, because . . . well, here I am.

In order to gather an understanding of my mother and my own birth story, I've had to endure some TMI moments with Dad and his wife of thirty years, Kristy. The tale is as old as time: Rod wasn't in love with Dee Dee, but he was brought up with a sense of duty that told him he had to marry her. It was the right thing to do when you get a girl pregnant. They had sex three times in their entire relationship and didn't consummate their marriage. Dee Dee didn't fuss too much about that. Maybe she had gotten what she wanted out of Rod already.

Because he was a minor, Dad needed his own mother's signature to consent to his marriage. The ceremony and reception were at the VFW in Golden Meadow, Louisiana, on December 27,

1990. On the way there, Dad and one of his groomsmen got in a wreck and totaled Mama's Ford Fiesta. Dad was arrested for driving without a license, and he used his phone call to ask Mama's parents, Claude and Emma, to bail him out so he could make it to the hall to marry their daughter. Once they all arrived at the altar, Dad didn't have the rings. In the middle of the ceremony my dad's best man, Terry Jr., literally ran out of the VFW and all the way back to Grandma Sharon's house to fetch the rings from the kitchen counter.

After the wedding reception, Dad and Mama partied at the Greenhouse, where Dad was chatting up his high school friends and old girlfriends and did a shot at the bar with his best friend, Kristy, who worked at the same local hospital as Mama. Kristy had been invited to the wedding but declined, saying she had other plans, a lie Kristy was caught in awkwardly as Mama ran into her at the Greenhouse. Dad looked handsome in his all-white tux, which had become playfully disheveled, with his shirt untucked and his tie unknotted. His mission: get drunk as a skunk. Which he did. Mission accomplished.

Mama and Dad's wedding night was spent in Claude and Emma's house, in the upstairs bedroom, where they planned to live for a while. At the age of seventeen, my dad was already working as a full-time fisherman, trawling for shrimp. He had signed himself out of high school as soon as he legally could to follow his own father's footsteps in the family trade. Trawling is a type of commercial fishing that involves a boat pulling a weighted fishing net behind it through the water or on the seafloor to target certain fish and seafood species, including a Louisiana staple, shrimp. My dad worked on a shrimp boat with twenty-foot nets that had mouths as large as Moby Dick's, swallowing up shrimp wherever they were hiding: in lakes, rivers, causeways, and the Bayou.

Trawling is hard work, especially when emptying the shrimp from the nets and putting them on ice and storing them. Dad would be gone for weeks at a time. Even today, his job as a boat captain requires him to work the boat for a month straight. At least once Mama had me, she'd have the help of her own mama while Dad was gone.

Being away from home so much made it convenient for Dad to play around behind Mama's back. Seeing other women without getting caught is a lot easier when you aren't expected home, and Dad went a little overboard (no pun intended) with his affairs. Ultimately, he got caught when a young girl around the same age as my dad came around looking for Mama's help, or at least that's the story Mama told me. The girl wanted money from Mama for an abortion because Rod had gotten her pregnant.

My mother, being Catholic, was not pro-choice, and said she wouldn't aid this stranger in getting an abortion. But she did have extra diapers and formula of mine that she'd give her to help. The other girl decided to have and keep the baby, and today I have a half sister almost the same age as me who doesn't live too far away.

She seems like a really great girl, raised by her mama and stepdad, whom she considers her father. She reached out to me once when I was in prison. She was gracious and kind to me. And I only wish her the very best and only happiness. Sorry—it's hard not to digress in my storytelling, as the more I investigate, the more the twists and turns of my colorful family unwind.

With the other woman out of the picture, Dad and Mama were still having a bit of a sex problem, in that they weren't having any. They hadn't officially consummated their marriage, and with Dad away so much and seeing other women, the last time they'd had sex was when I was conceived. My dad went back and forth on how to leave Mama, starting almost immediately after the wedding.

For almost three months, Rod called Kristy, asking for advice for a way out of the marriage. Over and over again he said to her, "I want to leave Dee Dee, but I don't know what to tell her."

"Tell her the truth, tell her how you feel," was Kristy's answer.

Rod even went to Kristy's mom for help, since she'd watched him grow up. Finally, on the morning of his eighteenth birthday, March 25, 1991, my dad packed his things while Mama slept.

"What you think you're doing?" she asked when the rustling awakened her, pulling the blankets off and sitting up.

"Dee Dee, I'm leaving. I don't love you. This is wrong, and I did this for the wrong reasons."

Without words, Mama popped up from her bed, ripped the framed marriage license off the wall, and threw it across the room.

I don't think this is when my mother's man hating began. I think she always hated them.

"Men might be nice to look at," she'd say, "but they'll betray you in a heartbeat. Better to just stay away from them all."

So I did. Until I didn't.

THREE

Cher

Term of endearment; "love" or "dear"

My father was not present at my birth. As I wrestled my way out of my mama, he was getting wasted and tripping on acid with his friends for four days at the Tarpon Rodeo, a fishing tournament over on Grand Isle. Minutes old and swaddled sweetly, I imagine my gaze enchanting my mother with a love and a fixed attention she had never known. And that's when she decided I was not to be shared.

When they cut the cord that connected us, defensively she held me tighter. It was just me and Mama "against the world," she'd say. From the get-go. Even when my dad decided, very soon after my birth, that he would "give it another go with Dee Dee and try to make it work" and moved us all into a rented house not far from

Claude and Emma. I appreciate the fact that my dad, still so young and carefree, would love me enough to attempt to give me a family he thought I deserved. But he and Mama still couldn't be intimate together, with my dad unable to talk himself into feeling a romantic love for Mama he never had. So he left her a second time, this time for good.

My dad gave us financial support, but let's face it, he was still a kid, and whatever he strung together didn't help my mother afford the rented house. So she asked her parents if she and I could move in and stay with them for a while, until my mother could get on her own feet. She had quit the hospital, where she'd worked as a nurse's aide.

"We told you you shoulda never got pregnant and you shoulda never married Rod in the first place," Mommzie Emma said, adding a click of the tongue for good measure. "But fine, you can stay here."

That's when Mama and I moved back to the Blue House, where we would live until I was about five years old.

After my arrest, my story swept the world as an egregious example of Munchausen syndrome by proxy, a psychological condition in which a parent or caregiver claims their dependent, typically a child, has a nonexistent illness. But I see now that my upbringing encompassed way more dysfunction than that. My mother's possessiveness tortured me as equally as the faked illnesses and unneeded surgeries. I'm still peeling back the layers that reveal elements of control and complete domination, which she established using several techniques over multiple domains of my life, not just my health care. I don't want to believe she was conscious of her ways. It's so hard to believe that. At the same time, I am haunted by the possibility that perhaps she *did* have awareness of the depth of the emotional pain she was causing, and simply lacked empathy for me. If she knew my pain, empathized with how it might feel to be locked away, prodded, and lied to, she wouldn't have done it in the first place, right? And if she couldn't put herself in my shoes and feel what I felt, does that mean she also didn't feel bad about it?

To possess someone, you must see them not as a person but as an object, like property. The literal meaning of possession is to physically take over the property. From that first gaze in the hospital, it was me and Mama against the world. No bad men, no intruders. My birth certificate was her deed to a property rightfully hers. The takeover had begun.

Before it was a physical takeover in the form of controlling my body's functions, it was an emotional one. I grew up dreamy eyed for Mama. When you're little, your world is so small. I had my mother, my bedroom, and my dolls. I was a sucker for dolls. My early memories are of my mother promising a new doll to me if I would just . . . see a new doctor, have a new procedure, nod in agreement, not ask "why," hold my tongue. Many say Mama was manipulative, holding the dolls over me like that. But getting the doll was *my* endgame, so wasn't I a willing participant? I was too young at that time for me to blame myself now, but I do wonder if I helped my mother do the things she did—to me, to the system, and to my dad.

Dolls were commerce, clauses in a long-term agreement between my mom and me, but they were also a symbol of innocence and purity. Mama preferred that I not play with Barbie dolls. She didn't want me to see the anatomy, no matter how poorly scaled, of a woman. If I were to undress a doll to change its clothes, I was to see a baby's body—without bulges or bumps. "Clean," she'd call it. The accessories for a baby doll were a baby bottle and a stroller, not a provocative hot tub or a dream house. The baby doll's companion was its mommy—not a Ken doll, which would've prompted more questions my mother didn't want to address.

I wonder: if I'd had the opportunity for Ken to play with Barbie, would my mother have known about Daddy Claude sooner?

At first, the shame she inflicted was subliminal, like implying that our natural naked state is dirty, by preferring "clean." But soon enough Mama became more literal in what she expected from my body: breasts were sinful and were to be covered, pubic hair was dirty and should be shaved off. Now, as I write this, I wonder if that kind of brainwashing about my sexuality was really a means to get me to be complicit in hiding my puberty from the outside world, to keep me young and consistent with her documentation. Regardless, for much of my life I felt confused and conflicted about my womanhood.

As I do the work of remembering the timeline of my life with her, imagining our first moments together in the maternity ward, being dressed as her mini me, being drafted into a united front against a family she for whatever reason felt ostracized from, I don't feel hatred toward my mother. I've come to see that my mother wanted me to keep my world small, as small as a child's, possibly because as hers became bigger and bigger, she got scared away. In my memories from between five and nine years old, our relationship felt like an innocent love, surrounded by toys resembling the small world, not the real world—Fisher Price Little People with their barreled bodies in their little cars in my little living room in a little Section 8 apartment in the Golden Meadow projects, where we moved after we left the Blue House, after Mommzie Emma died and Daddy Claude decided to marry Laura, a local nurse who had worked with Mama, and who Daddy Claude had a long-standing relationship with.

In the confines of our home, I never called my mom "Mama," at least not very often. And she rarely called me "Gypsy." Names have history; they're bigger than nicknames. Nicknames reduce a person to one small trait: safe and definable. Around the house, as I watched *The Lion King* for the hundredth time or pretended to feed kibble to my stuffed Rajah tiger from *Aladdin*, my mother called me "Baby," and I called her "Honey."

Honey and Baby were safe and had no past. My mother's love was in the present, and not small at all.

She was my Honey and I was her Baby. Our terms of endearment could be easily swapped with those of a newlywed couple intoxicated by each other's pheromones. "Honey," I'd call out to her, with my arm outstretched and bottle in hand, "more, Honey, more."

I see now I was her emotional support surrogate very early on, our dynamic resembling a couple instead of a mother-daughter duo. I'm all for the idea of "us against the world" if you are a fierce single mom, raising strong daughters, modeling what can be accomplished when you stick together. But our "us against the world" looked more like her sticking to me. While I was very young, that stickiness was sweet like molasses. "No one's ever going to take as good care of you as me, Baby," she'd say.

Molasses, if it's stored right, can last for years before it begins to mold over.

And for years we were each other's companions. We bathed together, slept in the same bed together, watched the same daytime television programs. Her interests in sci-fi and fantasy and *The People's Court* became my interests. When I showed my own curiosity for things separate from her, like Barbie dolls, she'd be there to deflect: "Now, you don't want those dolls when you have so many stuffed animals to play with."

I don't want Barbie.

There's power in numbers. And in my mother's paranoid, defensive mind, it had always been Claude and his other five children against Dee Dee, especially after Mommzie Emma passed. She and her brothers and sisters were like the neighboring towns of Lafourche Parish, stacked one right after the next, separated by invisible boundary lines that kept them out of each other's borders. One of Mama's brothers brought his invisible limit line out in clear view when he kicked us out of our own home. After Mommzie Emma died, Claude moved out of the Blue House and bought a new home with his second wife, Laura, leaving just me and Mama living in the Blue House. But Mama told me that my uncle claimed Mommzie Emma had verbally promised him that he'd get the house after she died. And he wanted what was rightfully promised to him.

So one day, after Mama and I came home from one of my doctors' appointments, we found all of our stuff out on the front porch and lawn. I remember seeing my uncle Pookie and Mama yelling at each other on the porch. My mama told me that my uncle and his wife and kids had moved in and kicked Mama and me out. "We're officially homeless," she said. Even though I was about five years old, I still remember feeling unsafe when I saw my favorite toys and dolls and nightgowns strewn out on the lawn like that. I wasn't yet in the wheelchair, but Mama already had doctors treating me for asthma, sleep apnea, hearing and vision impairments, and epilepsy, which she claimed were caused by a chromosomal deficiency, and she had taken me out of kindergarten to be homeschooled.

In a later conversation with Uncle Pookie, he explained to me that the argument he and Mama had on the porch was sparked by him questioning my mother about my mysterious bad health, telling her, "She needs to be in school, Dee Dee. Why is she not being schooled?" Never one to be told what to do, my mother did what she did best—ran away from those who had my best interest at heart, just because she couldn't handle being told she was wrong. Nobody told Mama she was wrong, not even the doctors.

I anticipate I will continue to uncover thousands of lies that pixelate the reality my mother designed for me, as if I'd been living in a simulation all those years.

For a short period of time after we were "kicked out," Mama and I stayed at her godmother's house, but we soon got kicked out of there, too, since, I later learned, Mama was caught stealing checks out of her godmother's checkbook. I don't know if she was that desperate for money or if she was just wanting to steal, but right after that we bounced to New Orleans for a while, where we lived rent free for weeks in the Ronald McDonald House. You're not supposed to stay so long. Once we were approved, we finally moved to the Golden Meadows projects, where I lived until I was nine.

Mama knew how to get approved for a lot of things and lived off the system, so I'm not sure if remanding me to a wheelchair was part of the scheme or if it was a symptom of her Munchausen by proxy. Mama scored three different government-issued phones, because she applied for different benefits for different reasons. We lived in Section 8 housing. We were both on Medicaid.

I was confined to a wheelchair after I was in a motorcycle accident when I was eight years old. Daddy Claude had a Harley, and I went riding one day on the back. Reacting to a car that had cut us off, Daddy Claude swerved out of the way and sideswiped us off the road. I was bleeding when we returned to Mama. After she found out what had happened, she rushed me to the hospital, where I was cleared of anything other than road rash.

I went home with an Ace bandage, and she nursed me as if I had had an amputation. She bought me a walker, sent me for physical therapy, and after a few months, came home with a wheelchair, which I was relegated to permanently. I learned recently that Mama's family members got on Mama for putting me in the wheelchair, but that only made her run away with me. At first, she told people I lost use of my legs from the accident. But as we moved around, her stories became more elaborate. She told some people my imaginary seizures damaged the motor function part of my brain. She was real strict when it came to me being still, which is why I was never allowed out of the wheelchair even in the privacy of our home. I had to maintain the habit. By the time I was in my teens, she harped on me: "Gypsy, I see you moving your legs," she'd say with a rap to my knee. "Stop moving them."

Mama's health was not the best, as she often reminded me, especially when she wanted to get me to behave or do something I didn't want to do. "You know I'm not feeling well, Baby. Why you sassin' me?" She said she was bipolar and had schizophrenia, but it's unclear whether those were legitimately diagnosed. I did bear witness to her frightening highs and lows.

Her type 2 diabetes, which was medically documented, required her to take insulin. It wasn't odd for a woman of her size who lived on Pepsi and milk, and who thought having to drink water was a punishment, to have diabetes. She was on pain meds because the fusion she had in her leg after a car accident never fully took, causing her chronic debilitating pain. All paid for by disability and social security.

With me playing the role of the sick child who required government checks and help from charities, and her own compromised health, Mama held me as her shield, her weapon against ever needing her family's assistance again. And she sent Daddy Claude a crystal-clear message to that effect. My mother and I attended his wedding ceremony to Laura dressed all in black.

FOUR

Tebecbo

Give me a sweet little kiss.

My mother always warned me to stay away from men. Now I knew why.

He was touchy-feely, and I thought that's what grandpas were supposed to be—affectionate, close, like a daddy, except smelling a little staler. As I've mentioned, for about five years of my childhood that I remember, I lived with the Pitre side of the family, my mother moving back into the Blue House in Golden Meadow, where she'd grown up with Daddy Claude and Mommzie Emma. Following the incident with my uncle, we'd move to the projects and then, after a car accident, in with Daddy Claude and his new wife, Laura.

It is no secret, nor is it an exaggeration, to say that my mother and Laura hated each other, and for reasons I am not sure of. Family members have said that my mother freaked out because Claude remarried so quickly after Mommzie Emma passed at age fifty-nine, and therefore my mother had it out for Laura by default. But Laura had an equally passionate disdain for my mother, allegedly acting out against her at the hospital where they worked together.

According to what Mama told me, Laura once opened Mama's work locker and stole Mama's wedding picture, ripped it in half and tore up just Mama's face and body into a million little pieces, and then put them all back inside the locker for Mama to find. Mama thought Laura and her whole relationship with Daddy Claude was inappropriate.

I agree with my mother that Daddy Claude was inappropriate, but not because he replaced his wife.

Many of my family members, including Claude himself, deny that there had ever been any sexual abuse at Claude's hands. In a TV documentary, he offered an implausible counter-narrative: "She was the one trying to touch me, and I'd say no, don't do that. She started doing that when she was about four years old." My mother's credibility is obviously in question, and her being an unreliable narrator helps support the reasonable doubt that outsiders have. But I know what I saw, what I witnessed, and what I felt.

On the second floor of the Blue House, there was a bathroom. I can still see the white claw-foot tub and the black-and-white checked floors. I was about five years old and sitting on the toilet watching Daddy Claude and my mother step their naked bodies into the tub. My mother at almost thirty years old was a lot skinnier back then. Father and daughter trying to fit into the small tub together reminded me of those miniature circus cars filled with an illogical number of clowns.

My mother and Claude had an intentional bath time. It wasn't like she'd already be in the tub and he'd decide to join her. They went into the room together and undressed. The whole nine. After my mother was done washing Daddy Claude's back and she turned so he could do hers, she'd call to me, "It's your turn," and she'd get out of the tub and undress me, carry me over, and plop me in the water.

"We'll need to wash that pecan of yours," Claude said as he lathered soap on his hands, my mother leaving the bathroom, only to check on us intermittently. At five years old, I didn't think much of him cleaning my pecan.

The baths stopped after we managed to move into subsidized housing in Golden Meadow, just a turn from the Blue House. But when I was about eight or nine years old, my mother and I were in a car accident. She was in the hospital for two months. Her tibia and fibula were broken, and she needed to have plates and rods and screws put in, which never resulted in the bone fusion her doctors had hoped for. Afterward, she experienced chronic pain, which led her to be prescribed pain meds, which led to my addiction to her opioids. In order to help her recover and care for me, we moved in with Claude and Laura in their new house.

While she recuperated for several months, my mother and I slept on a pull-out couch in the living room. I remember Daddy Claude moseying over like an ole grizzly bear to where I was lying. His hand moved toward my pull-up diaper like it was a pot of honey. Mom's arm swiftly intervened. Like human fly swatter, she shooed Daddy's hand away. He grunted and walked out of the room. Her message to keep his hands off was too late. Daddy had already crossed a line that should never have been approached.

While my mother was in the hospital after her leg surgery, I was cared for by Laura, who was a former nurse, and Daddy Claude. They were vigilant with my medication doses and knew how to administer food through my feeding tube. (I had a permanent feeding tube that was attached to my abdomen when I was about nine years old, soon after the motorcycle accident with Daddy Claude. Unlike the portrayal in *The Act*, my mother never blended real food and fed it to me through the tube. My feeding tube was used strictly to administer water, liquid nutrition supplements, and medications. When I got to county jail, I weighed ninety-two pounds at almost twenty-four years old, due to a daily menu of PediaSure and other electrolyte drinks.)

Since I was pulled out of any formal school around pre-K age, my days were wide open, with me and Daddy Claude cuddling up on the couch to watch *The Price Is Right*. On rainy days I'd stay in my PJs, and on sticky hot days, I'd lounge in just a T-shirt.

Being with Daddy Claude filled a void I felt but didn't know how to articulate. I knew from watching television that kids had moms and dads. I knew that technically I had a dad, but he didn't live with us, and my mother had told me he was very busy with his new children. I craved the kind of attention a dad might give his little girl. Claude—with his arm around me, and me curled in a side ball resting my head on his chest—was my daddy, so that's what I called him.

The grazing of his hand along my clothes was deceptively innocent at first. We'd call out to the game-show contestants on television "one hundred dollars" for convection ovens and juicers and insist on them choosing "door number two." I'd hardly notice Daddy's finger tracing circle shapes on my shoulder or my waist. The touch would linger in ways that made me uncomfortable, though I didn't fully understand why. I was not even close to puberty, and sex was not yet a discussion. *This is a Daddy's love,* was really what I thought. *Daddies take bath time with their daughters.*

One day while watching TV, Daddy Claude scooped me up from where I was lying on the couch. "I want to show you something, Possum." He carried me toward his bedroom, where Laura was napping. She had frequent fainting spells that would knock her out, so Daddy walked us past her bed and, like a groom carrying his bride over the threshold took me into the walk-in closet. He turned the light on, shut the door, and deposited me on top of a plastic dresser, like the ones you see in Walmart, with clear drawers and white casing. Anyway, I sat in my nightgown and asked, "What is it?"

He pulled my nightgown above my knees and spread them apart with his hands. I didn't resist. Mama would've killed me if she found out I moved my legs in front of anyone, even close family.

I inhaled the woodiness of the Brut cologne he wore as I felt the coldness of air on the bare parts of my private place. I was a child. Far too young to understand or consent. The experience was confusing, uncomfortable, and would leave lasting trauma.

The threshold he had crossed me over became the Rubicon as he carried me back out to the couch, a giver of a love I no longer wanted. "They could arrest me for this, Possum," he said. But as usual, no adults would notice or rescue me.

During a two-hour trip to New Orleans, about a year later, I decided to tell my mother what Daddy Claude did. "I have something to tell you, Mama," I said, while she held the wheel of the car steady. "Daddy Claude touched me."

Tears streamed down her face, as if she knew exactly what I meant. She bluntly asked, "Did he put his finger inside you?"

"No, Mama," I said, scared of how sad I had made her, regretful of my decision to tell.

"It wasn't anything, Mama, don't worry," I added, reassuring her with my backtracking.

The subject didn't come up again until almost a decade later, when I was about nineteen. I asked my mother why she didn't have a boyfriend or a new husband. "I don't want a man in my life, not after what your father did to me and not after Claude ..."

She began to cry and detailed how Claude had molested her. I cried with her, letting out all of my emotions about all those years he abused me, bonding my confusion with hers. It was one of the only authentic moments I ever had with my mother. It was the only time I ever heard her say to me, "I'm so sorry."

FIVE

Pauvre Ti Bête

Poor little thing

My mother limited my interactions with others as much as possible. I was a Daisy in the Girl Scouts, but when it was time to graduate to become a Brownie, I got stuck there, never becoming a Junior. My mom volunteered for the Girl Scouts, but we changed troops a lot, always starting over. Because my exposure to anyone other than my mother was so limited, I had no idea that the way I lived was different or unusual. How could I?

I attended school for one year—kindergarten. After that, Mama pulled me out to homeschool me. Except that was a lie. She didn't register me as a homeschooler with either state that I lived in. No school officials seemed to notice. I remember when we'd see new doctors and the intake forms asked where I went to school, Mama would just list the local school I was zoned for. That was that. Nobody followed up or questioned us. Everyone who hears my story is appalled at the medical institutions failing me, but the education system was actually the first to let me fall through the cracks.

Without a broader range of exposure to how others lived their lives, I didn't suspect that our daily schedule was odd or dysfunctional:

We woke up each day at around 11 A.M.

I'd have my medicines.

At the start of my day, my mother usually slammed a sealed tube of Pillsbury biscuits against the countertop to pop it open, and she baked them on a baking sheet for breakfast. I always thought the way she made the pop sound was like magic. When the whole house smelled buttery, she'd prepare my PediaSure and meds and administer them to me through the feeding tube. She would eat the biscuits herself.

We'd watch *The Bold and the Beautiful*.

We would only get dressed if we had to run an errand.

We'd watch a movie if there wasn't an errand to run.

She didn't eat meat, so most of the time she made sweet peas over rice for her dinner.

We would watch another movie.

Then we'd start our night routine: She'd bathe me, dress me, and put me into our bed. Technically, I had my own bed in my own bedroom, but ever since I could remember, I slept on the left side of my mother's bed. Next, she'd turn on my breathing machine, which actually didn't help me breathe at all. Then she'd turn out the lights.

My routine was all I had, but it never included going to school or outside to play. The times I spent outside were so few and far between that I remember each one vividly. I was a very lonely child. When I was young, maybe up to age fourteen, I thought I could make friends with other kids who were like me. With other Make-a-Wish kids or other wheelchair-bound kids I would compete against in the GUMBO games, which was Louisiana's smaller version of the Special Olympics. I remember one girl who I saw a lot at these events. She had spina bifida and was always accompanied by a home health aide. But then Mama moved us away, and we didn't see each other after that.

With all my arts and crafts, I would trace and cut out circles and squares and long rectangles, and I'd piece together life-size paper people and sit them on my couch with me. Sometimes I would make several of them and have a playgroup in my house. Being flanked by the paper people while watching TV made me feel less alone, like I belonged to a community, even if it was an imaginary one. I had a rubber pet rat, the kind they sell during Halloween time. I even had a friend that was a snowman.

One glorious memory I have playing with Mama was when we first moved to Aurora, Missouri, before we were blessed to receive our Habitat for Humanity house. It was our first winter experience. Being from Louisiana, seeing snow was like someone shook the snow globe I lived inside, making me a princess in a little kingdom of cottony dreams.

Mama and I built a snowman and we named him Frosty, the Mardi Gras Snowman. Like I said, Mama was all about her culture. Her Cajun spice melted the snow that day. We laughed and threw snowballs, me sitting in the snow, my legs frozen by her command, my heart warmed by the icicles crying blue droplets in the low light of the winter sun.

We didn't even own a shovel. After one big snowstorm blocked the walkway to our door, a neighbor yelled across the yard to us, holding up a shovel, "Hey, you're going to need one of these!" We all laughed because only people who had never seen snow before would glorify the mess. Soon enough we learned like everyone else to dread the aftermath of a wintery wrath.

In terms of winter festivities, that one snowman-building episode is all I have in my memory bank. Mama and I didn't celebrate Christmas or any other national holidays with anyone else. I mean, she gave me presents on Christmas, but it was never celebrated with family. Food and festive music and tradition were not things Mama infused in our routine. I never had the joy of a family meal or a New Year's Eve celebration.

I wondered a lot about what Dad and Kristy and the kids were up to, especially on New Year's Eve. I didn't know my dad very well, since we only saw each other once a year, at best. Mama had moved me so far away from them, and Dad's job took him out of town a lot. I have tiny, random memories of us at the mall, and one of my little brother, Dylan, and me at Walmart. He bought a Star Wars lightsaber and I got a baby doll. Kristy and Dad came to one of my wheelchair races once, but I didn't see them or talk to them much beyond that handful of visits. But I did know Dad was fun-loving because he made me laugh and had a lot of energy. I imagined them having New Year's Eve parties with neighbors and lots of music.

I pushed away the thoughts of the other family I had some-where, and we watched the ball drop in Times Square on television, Mama and me, while we heard horns and clacking cowbells of the world outside—from inside our dark and gloomy snow globe.

Like all worlds, our globe had its own rules, except our rules defied reality. In our world, you didn't have to be a baby to wear diapers or use bottles. In our world, you didn't use maxi pads or tampons during your period. You wore Pull-Ups. In our world, the hair on your head was as filthy as the hair on your vagina, and both places should be shaved clean.

From the time I was born to when I was month shy of twenty-four years old, Mama had never weaned me off the bottle. The baby bottle was my safety blanket, my security that I turned to when I was nervous before a doctor's appointment or surgery, a sooth-ing mechanism to help me sleep, or just a comfort and companion when I would watch television or draw. It was filled with PediaSure (strawberry flavor was my favorite), and I would stick the bottle underneath my armpit to warm it up. I was extremely picky when it came to the nipples of the bottles. I didn't like the brown ones and preferred the clear nipples because they controlled the flow better, in my opinion. I didn't like the fluid to come out too fast. I preferred the bottle to the feeding tube, of course, because I got to enjoy the taste of the nourishment.

My sucking on the bottle wasn't a secret. We packed it up like you would a diaper bag when we ran errands. Of course, people would look sideways at first at a thirteen-year-old whipping out her bottle, but Mama would remind them, "She's very mentally slow," or, "It's one of the two ways she can get her sustenance." To which people always replied with a nod. *Yes, of course, makes total sense.*

As a result of my late-stage bottle sucking, I developed the same teeth as SpongeBob SquarePants. And all my remaining teeth were ultimately extracted, for a reason I still don't know.

For public appearances, like when we were being interviewed by a newspaper reporter or at a charity event, Mama brought my sippy cup. That was another method of my nourishment, in use right up until I got arrested. I had several sippy cups with Buzz Lightyear, Elsa, and Nemo on them.

This was all so normal to me. Sitting there on the rug of our home, sucking away sweetly, until one day my normal was disrupted by an abnormal flow. Around the time I was thirteen, about a year before Hurricane Katrina, I was sitting on the floor in the living room of our apartment in Slidell, Louisiana, playing with dolls and watching *The Little Mermaid*. I noticed something wet and maroon colored beneath me, so dark I thought I was sitting in barbeque sauce at first. I lifted myself into my wheelchair and called for Mama, crying that something was wrong with me.

"You're bleeding, Baby," she said, as if she were expecting my bottom to fall out like that. "Okay, this is what's going to happen to you, you're going to bleed like that for a good part of your life."

That was about all the knowledge I would get from her about a period. She never even called it a period, or menses, or anything like that. She just kept saying graphically, "You're gonna bleed." That's when she left the room and returned with a clean Pull-Up. "Here," she said. "Let's get you changed and try to get you as clean as we can."

"Bleeding will happen to you." To this day, I wish I had more motherly words to keep in my head every time my time of the month comes. I wish Mama could have been a mother in that moment and explain to me how blessed I am to have a regular period, because I will reproduce one day, make life—a sacred superpower. She made me feel the opposite of special, speaking of menstruation with a tone of gore and disgust. I remember when I first saw the movie *Carrie* in prison, and the mom in that movie was so warped when it came to Carrie's monthly, I felt oddly connected. *Oh my God, that mother is just like my mother!* I thought.

My mother lied to doctors all the way into my later teen years, saying that I never got my first period. That was very concerning to all of them. We needed to undergo another battery of tests. Maybe my pituitary gland was the problem, or maybe they should look at my bladder for good measure. To test my bladder and urine, I had a catheter inserted four times, which is so painful. I never asked her why the lies about this, especially when we both knew that I bled every month on schedule. I was just never a "why" kind of kid. And I didn't want to steal her thunder. I saw how she soaked in the attention and limelight, even though it was only local. Beyond the interpersonal attention, in the form of the sympathy and martyrdom she delighted in, she basked in the bright spotlight when the cameras rolled. "Turn on the news!" she'd say to someone she had called on the phone. "Pick up this Sunday's paper . . . you'll never guess who's in it!" she'd tease with stars in her eyes.

The notoriety added a dimension to her disease. Yes, the Munchausen syndrome by proxy was the most dangerous part of the abuse, but it also acted as a backstage pass to my mother's internal cinematic show. Whatever that movie in her mind was, I wasn't the star of it. Mama's friend from high school said, "Your mama wanted to be famous. She wanted to marry a rock star or an actor." When the press arrived, Mama would be doing all of the talking, while I numbly waited for my cue. Like a stage mother, Beauty Queen Dee Dee fed me my lines: "It's a dream come true," "This makes me so happy," "My mom is my best friend." Through me and through the script we memorized, Mama could achieve some level of the fame she had long desired.

Even when nobody was there, the act was still on and the script was still in play. When my dad would call me, she became just like one of those stage moms or dance moms, mouthing lines or counting cadence. I never had a moment alone on the phone with my father, nor an authentic conversation. She always hovered. I can't imagine how my dad must have felt knowing that every time he wanted to check in with me, my mother was the first line of defense. He had to get through her, and sometimes he didn't. When she answered his call, she'd set up the expectation for how the call would go by saying something like, "She's tired today," or, "We are about to run errands." So, like an official at a football game, she set the clock.

After she preempted the conversation, she'd hand me the phone, me in my wheelchair pulling the cord on the landline, saying an awkward hello to this man who I, at that time, only referred to as "my father," instead of "dad." "Dad" felt too casual and comfortable and familiar for the long-distance relationship we had.

"Tell him about the new doll I bought you," Mama whispered before I could say anything beyond hello.

"Hi, ummm, Mama bought me a new doll for being brave at the doctor's yesterday."

"Wow, you're a lucky girl, Gypsy," Dad answered. "What did you name her?"

Already bored and too far from her agenda, Mama continued her prompt: "Tell him that I stayed up with you all night last week because of your fever."

"I had a fever last week," I parroted, "and Mama stayed up all night with me. We were so tired."

My dad cleared his throat, and said, "Well, I always tell Dee Dee she does a fine job being your mama."

Then Mama would move around to face me and whisper, "Alright, that's enough. Tell him we're about to leave."

"Well, ummm, I have to go now; we have to leave."

When Dad and I'd hang up, he'd say "I love you" and I'd say the same, parroting him, as I wasn't sure we actually could know each other well enough to love each other. Mama would look at me twisted, as if I were a pretty roommate who was after her boyfriend. Like I was the competition. Is that why she kept me ugly and infantilized? If I came of age, would I be prettier or skinnier or win the crown at the pageant instead of her? She'd grab one of the cats and baby talk with it, loving on her, and talking about me as if I weren't in the room. "C'mon, Tebecbo. Give your mama a sweet little kiss."

More often, after we hung up, Mama would bad-mouth my dad for a long time. She loved him so much, she hated him. Her disgust for my father was the reason, she told me, that she kept my hair so short as a child. "Ugh, when your hair is longer, you look just like your father," she'd say, spewing venom. I never felt too bad for him, because I was well aware from Mama of what a bad person he was. His poor new children were now the ones being abused. Mama would never put up with his abuse. I felt very lucky she protected me from him all those years.

Getting attention and drawing it are two different things. Maybe she thought conversations like this earned her accolades from outsiders, especially my dad. Or telling others about the non-existent abuse at the hands of my father made her even braver, more of a feminist. But when she got the attention of Child Protective Services, my mother deflected the attention instead of embracing it.

I was not drugged the day the woman from the Department of Family Services (DFS) gave us a surprise visit on October 26, 2009. I've been told *The Act* portrayed it that way; I still haven't found it necessary to watch the series. The truth is, I was still quite trusting of my mother at this time. The way I remember it, we were watching television in the bedroom together when the doorbell rang. I was so excited. We never had guests, especially surprise ones, so I remember eagerly wheeling out to the door and being the one to answer it. When I opened the door, I was met by two women from DFS and a deputy sheriff.

"Is your mother here?" asked one of the visitors.

"Yes."

Mama walked out as on cue, and the DFS officers said, "Ma'am, can you come out to the front porch, please?"

She did, and the four of them talked outside for a few minutes, and then returned to the living room, where I was interviewed. I get how this has become another situation that people ask about with frustration: "Why didn't you tell them anything when you had the chance?"

I didn't think my life was odd at that time. This was before I had access to a laptop, and boys, and widened my lens on what reality should look like. Mama and I went to the movies and stayed up at night to talk about *Brave* or whatever new movie was being hyped. Sometimes, we slept in a tent together in the middle of the living room. She'd hold a flashlight in front of her face, like in *The Blair Witch Project,* and make me laugh with her spooky howls. The cat would join us and chase after the spotlight from the flashlight, making us both lovingly chuckle.

I look back now and I think maybe if DFS had asked the *right* questions, they might have sensed something was off. Their questions begged for negative answers.

"Are there any bruises on your body, Gypsy?"

"No." Because there weren't yet.

"Can we look at your legs and your arms, Gypsy?"

They did. They searched me for signs of physical abuse. They went to see my bedroom, where it looked like it had been decorated by a unicorn or something—pink and magical, princess sheets and stuffed animals galore.

"Tell us about your life, Gypsy," I remember being asked. From the DFS reports I now have, I see their visit was initiated by a hotline call from St. John's Hospital stating that a doctor could not find any symptoms that would support what my mother alleged was wrong with me. Further, the inconsistent information regarding my birth dates and other personal information as well as "lack of a medical diagnoses" prompted DFS to determine whether I was a runaway or a missing juvenile. They also wanted to ensure that Mama was my biological mother.

So while they focused on asking for Mama's driver's license and my social security card, I showed off my toys and dolls and dresses to them.

The report states that Mama told them she had been in a "bad marriage" and changed our names and locations to avoid my father. But in the same report it says, "When confronted about all the inconsistent information that she had provided to the hospital, Clauddine stated she didn't know why the birth dates and personal information were wrong."

So, which is it? She didn't know why the dates were wrong, or she changed them to avoid an abusive husband? The blatantly contradicting answers to the same question are so obvious to me as lies. But the investigators didn't seem to notice. Instead, the report continues, "DFS and I cleared the scene without further incident."

They never came back. Another institution that dropped the ball.

As each year passed and another surgery or painful test was performed, my childhood innocence began to be replaced with the ability to observe and make connections about my mother's behaviors and what she instructed me to do or say. After that DFS visit, Mama became paranoid about strangers. She disconnected our doorbell and made sure all of the windows had black trash bags over them. Equally weird was when I found my Medicaid card, which revealed my actual birth year of 1991. I was living a life in which I thought I was four years younger than I was. She told me it was a typo. I believed her. But I sensed the discrepancy shifting the tectonic plate of our private continent, separating us and allowing more suspicion to creep in.

I had been taught to live a life of lies and deception, an accomplice to my mother's fraud, which made me feel sinful and burdened with a feeling of filth. For a Catholic, guilt can keep you up nights. Catholicism and southern Louisiana go together like bread and butter. In Golden Meadow, everyone had a shrine to the Virgin Mary on their lawn. I was christened Catholic and grew up going to Catholic Mass every Sunday with my Daddy Claude and Mommzie Emma. Mama used to tell everyone, "Gypsy's going to be a nun when she grows up." Growing up near New Orleans, there was a strong Catholic influence, obviously the biggest being Fat Tuesday, or in French, Mardi Gras, which signified the beginning of Lent, the holiest time of the year that leads up to Easter, Christ's resurrection. But there was a flip side: the supernatural influence of voodoo and witchcraft; pagan rituals; tarot and fortune-telling.

When my mother put me in Vacation Bible School, where she'd work as a volunteer, she bought plastic mini statues of the saints, like St. Joseph and St. Agnes, from the gift shop. I already thought I was going to be a nun, so I made an altar in my bedroom, where I placed the saints. I aligned my stuffed animals as a congregation, along with my cats, and we'd all attend Little Church. I was the priest. I led us all in prayer and gave out Communion, feeding crackers and grape juice to my cats. After I started to get glimpses of Mama's true ways, I'd pray to God at my personal altar and at Sunday Mass to send me a blessing to make all the ickiness go away. No blessing came. No family members came. My father didn't come. The doctors didn't come. No teacher or principal came. DFS came and then left.

I was mad at God because I'd ask him in church, and before bed, and in my head, over and over, *God, make this tormenting hell stop. Please help.* But there was no help in sight, at least not in my sight.

SIX

Lagniappe

*A little something extra
you probably weren't expecting*

Everyone in Mama's family knew she was a hoarder. Before we arrived in Springfield, Missouri, when I was fifteen years old, we had been traveling light. With just the clothes in our suitcases and a few of our favorite things—my mother's baby pillow and my stuffed blue dog, ingeniously named Blue Doggie—we bounced around from the time I was eight. I imagine that without a permanent place for my mother to store all her emotional baggage, she doubled down on collecting physical baggage once we landed in Springfield, where we were blessed to receive our Habitat for Humanity house on Volunteer Way.

We frequented yard sales and bought crap just to buy it, like game consoles, souvenirs from other people's vacations, and even furniture we didn't need. It was mostly clothing she hoarded. My mother couldn't say no to a donation. She loved a good "going out of business" sale, even if the items on 90 percent markdown were useless to us. She was a shopaholic, for sure. Maybe this was another coping mechanism for dealing with her clinical depression. The days after holidays were her favorite time to run out to JCPenney or Dillard's to snatch up prom dresses after prom season ended; to Michael's to round up next year's Christmas decorations; or she'd buy merch for events after the fact, like a bicentennial celebration T-shirt a year after the fireworks show.

Then there were the things we'd steal. My mother taught me the art of shoplifting at a very young age. She had a family history of kleptomania, I found out very recently. Legend has it that my grandmother Emma had been arrested for stealing, and she had been caught and banned from food and clothing stores on more than one occasion. My mother grew up with a comfortable middle-class lifestyle, so any thievery must have been just for a high. Did Emma teach my mother how to steal, which is why Mama taught me how to?

While sometimes I believe we stole because she wanted to get me things that we simply couldn't afford, I also think she experienced a thrill from the satisfaction of knowing we pulled one over. I remember my mother stealing a wheelchair from the children's hospital in Kansas City. I'd just had surgery on my lazy eye—

a condition I actually had—and she wheeled me right out of the building and into our van. Later, she took nail polish remover and a toothbrush and scrubbed off the hospital's name. The hospital had trusted us to use the wheelchair until we got to the car. She loaded it into the car as nonchalantly as you would a bag of groceries, and we drove away. I imagined her thinking, *I wonder when or if they'll ever notice it's gone.*

We actually had several, maybe five, wheelchairs that sat throughout our small home. Like her pewter wizard figurines, my mother collected wheelchairs. We had a collapsible one, a Jazzy powered wheelchair, and another power wheelchair that was custom-made so everything from the seat to the hydraulics was fit for me. Medicaid paid for the custom power wheelchair. My mom paid for the travel wheelchair she bought at Target or Walmart. Insurance covered the Jazzy. As I grew older, my mother preferred me to use the foldable wheelchair, as it required her to push me and made me less independent.

Sitting in a wheelchair in the store aisles helped me more easily catch and conceal items my mother would knock into my lap. When she wasn't dressing me as a boy, I'd head to Walmart in my princess costume, the tulle of the skirt being a great canopy for hiding merchandise. And for items that couldn't be sat on or hidden underneath my beanie cap, my mother taught me the barcode swap: remove the barcode sticker from a cheaper item and place it on the more expensive one; then use the self-checkout lane. Since Sam's Club didn't have metal detectors, I'd be able to fit fourteen or fifteen CDs on me. We'd steal random stuff at Hobby Lobby, mostly arts-and-crafts items, which I used a lot of. My outlet was drawing and painting and making characters with those googly eyes you glue on and different-colored feathers. I also loved to sketch. When I went to prison, one of the items that I asked Dad and Kristy to save from the house was my book of artwork.

But one time, we tripped an alarm at Hobby Lobby. And as if they had been waiting for this moment for a long time, the manager and a minion ran to where we were, just outside the door. "Search her," the manager said, pointing to me, in particular the part of my dress the crafts were crushed beneath. My mother put on her fake victim voice and acted all appalled, but they actually did it; they searched where I was seated in my wheelchair and discovered the gluey, sticky, sparkly contraband. We were marched to the back office, and I remember thinking what a cool job being the manager of a Hobby Lobby must be. How omnipotent the manager must feel, being able to watch people roam around his store from the one-way glass, none of them the wiser. How differently all the shoppers might act if they realized they were being observed. I knew how it felt to be looked at all the time, how to act when being observed, and like the shoppers in the store, I didn't have the power to look back. I wanted to have an advantage like the manager's, for once in my life.

Believe it or not, the police were called and charges were pressed. Mama and I were banned from ever returning to any Hobby Lobby in the entire country. At least that was my understanding. Mama was pissed because we had to hire an attorney and everything. But it didn't stop her from stealing from other stores, only to bring the goods home never to be used. I'd later learn that Mama had several charges against her in Louisiana, but they didn't follow when we left the state.

In Missouri, the bedroom where my mother and I slept had so much stuff piled in it, I needed to carve a pathway for myself from the door to the bed. My wheelchair barely fit through the door-way. In fact, we had to take our bedroom door off its hinges; there wasn't room for it to open completely, which made it impossible for me to wheel through without crashing into the doorframe.

You know those giant black bags you use to throw leaves and grass cuttings in? The ones that you can step in if you are shorter than five foot three, like me? They were everywhere, all filled with clothes. And, as if they were dresser drawers or filing cabinets, my mother knew the contents of each bag. She knew where every-thing was. The premiere of the new *Jurassic Park* movie is today? No problem. She'd head out to the shed or into the back bedroom and whip out a T-shirt with T-Rex on it.

She saved everything. I always wondered what she was afraid of losing. Whatever it was, it controlled her life. Beyond stealing and hoarding, my mother was being treated by a doctor for bipolar disorder. I was too small to take note whether the shopping sprees coincided with the mania that she'd experience for weeks on end. I couldn't keep up with her during her manic episodes. She'd stay up all night and clean, do the dishes, move the black bags of clothing around, and wash the clothes and fold them, only to put them back in the black plastic.

When she was depressed, Mama would cover the windows with black garbage bags and stay in bed for weeks at a time. After the DFS visit, the garbage bags became permanent. "Get up; get out of bed," I'd say, as I would try to roll her over and off the bed. "You can't stay asleep all the time; I'm hungry." She was receiving disability checks for her bipolar disorder, and once a week, a woman who worked for the social security office would make visits for therapy. It got to a point where my mother didn't want to talk to her anymore, so she stopped letting her in.

She took Xanax and Ambien to knock herself out, especially after something set her off. And it could be anything. A clerk at the checkout counter was rude to her, someone didn't return her phone call, she saw postings of Kristy and my dad on Facebook. She'd head straight to bed and wouldn't even get up to eat. When I was much younger, before I understood my life was totally abnormal, these episodes scared me sick. I would frantically figure out how to get food to her. I knew how to make toast, so I'd make a lot of it. Then I graduated to making Pillsbury biscuits in a toaster oven. Even in her despair, she'd set an alarm, and when it went off she'd give me my medicine and my feeding—because if she didn't, I might begin to see that nothing bad would happen to me.

When her bipolar condition was not controlled, she'd stop being my mother, which scared the shit out of me. Now I think that maybe she liked seeing me afraid because it showed I loved her. She needed that attention. Was this part of the game? The pulling one over on me, conning me so I'd care for her and fuss over her? She'd always say I was the only person she had in life. "You're my heart," she'd tell me. When we'd take baths together, she'd remind me how it's me and her against the world, forever. One time I noticed raised red marks on her arm. I remember rubbing my fingers along them, sprinkling bathwater over her as if the droplets would magically heal them. As I investigated the marks more closely, the word PAIN came into view, appearing like a film negative submerged into a basin of developing solution.

"That looks like it hurts," I said, appalled that she had carved the word "pain" into her forearm. How recently or long ago, I could not know.

"It relieves the pain," she said.

I swallowed my own hurt down, wanting to make her pain go away. So I bandaged her wounds for her, feeling a sense of purpose, when she said, "I help you, you help me; we take care of each other."

She threatened to kill herself on many occasions. "You know, Gypsy, I might look big like a rhino but I don't have the skin of one," she'd say.

As I grew older, I realized she was guilting me to control me. At first it was jarring to hear her blurt out, "I just want to die," because I was afraid of what would happen to me. We were all each other had, and I wanted to protect our little family. Over time, it became something she'd say when we were having a disagreement or I was sassing her.

On several occasions, I wanted to know why my mother didn't want someone other than me in her life to love her, make her feel special, and generally be her companion. I began to wish she had someone else, so she would loosen her grip on me, let me go a little. There would be men who asked my mom on a date. Her answer to them was always, "My focus is on my daughter."

"And why do you want me with a man so much, Baby?" she'd ask me, when I'd see a nice man in a hospital waiting room or at the Ronald McDonald House and nudge her, as a way to say, *Go talk to him.*

"I want a daddy," was always my reply.

"What can you get from a daddy that I can't give you?" she'd answer. We both knew it was a rhetorical question.

Was she using me as a shield? Or was inviting others into our lives going to increase the odds of someone finding us out, the same reason she kept me out of school and isolated me from her entire family? Had I been in school, I would hope that experienced educators would catch on that my IQ was not low, and a school nurse administering albuterol for asthma would realize real quick that my lungs filled up like balloons. Given the opportunity, someone at some point was bound to figure out that I was intelligent, mobile, and older than I thought. So my mother kept the circle small.

Behind closed doors, she'd blame her being alone all on me: "Your dad left me because of you."

When her shadow side came out during her depressive weeks, that blame turned to disdain, and she'd say her favorite line:

"There are eight personalities in my head, and seven of them don't like you."

On those days I'd try to find a place to hide in our small, little house, so to not further clutter her mind. But at nighttime, she'd still come for me, so I could lie all night with her seven hateful personalities.

"This is your fault, Gypsy."

"I do everything for you. I've sacrificed everything. And this is how you repay me?"

The hits kept coming, even as I pretended to sleep, muzzled with a CPAP machine, choking on my mother's contempt.

I even got blamed for her sisters not favoring her, which made it hard for me to form a relationship with all her siblings. My mother positioned a wall between me and her family, the Pitres, which is one of the reasons I didn't call them for help. Any failures in my mother's life were because of me.

Eventually there was no one else around to blame. We only had temporary friends, no consistent home, always starting over in a new place. She couldn't blame her family, who she estranged us from. And at this point, I had minimal contact with my dad. Her only constant was me.

SEVEN

Menteur

Liar

I didn't know I could think for myself until I began to search the internet with an HP notebook laptop. I was told the computer was a gift from the Leukemia & Lymphoma Society one Christmas when I was real-age eighteen; the charity thought I was just thirteen. We received a lot of help and gifts from charities along with government entitlements, like food stamps, disability checks, and Section 8 housing. It's a fact that makes my skin crawl.

I watched my mother maneuver her way around the system, craftily researching the help and even perks available to a "kid like me." I didn't know it was a scam until about a year after I found my Medicaid card with my correct birth date listed, when Mama became more physical and violent with me after I re-questioned her about it, pushing back against her storytelling. The discovery of my real birth date was not my "aha moment" per se, but it did act as a warning siren to be more alert and observe more closely.

Mama was a natural-born salesperson. She told me she sold phone books door-to-door, back when there were phone books. She was selling me a version of herself who worked like a dog after my father "left us," with only her to take care of me. But I see now, this has to be a lie. Phone books were left on people's doorsteps for free.

I do remember Mama bought a Gateway computer and started doing photo restoration with it. She had a little business where she would take old and scratched-up prints and fix them up real nice. She could cut and paste people into paintings, like this one time when she made Jesus the captain of a boat on stormy seas. Another one I remember was an image of her as a baby superimposed on a photograph of her holding me as a baby. I watched her print out numbers one through ten, and cut the numbers and paste them on a document and scan the document and print it out so that it looked official. She got really good at the cut-and-paste job, which makes me wonder now if her business *was* forgery, like helping kids get fake IDs or making fake social security cards to steal identities.

When it was time for our two-hour and forty-five-minute drive from Springfield to Children's Mercy Hospital in Kansas City to see my neurologist, cardiologist, pulmonologist, and allergist, my mother found help from charities that reimburse families for their gas money. Mama would buy gas and have those receipts and send them in so she'd get the reimbursement. At the same time, she'd book the same medical visit through Angel Flight, a program in which pilots donate their planes and their time to patients in need of medical or charitable care. So she'd take the cash for the gas reimbursement even though we were flying for free and not driving at all. Thinking about how cruel this was to do to the charities and the families who were actually in need makes me nauseous and regretful.

The lies continued when she began knocking back my age, which she started doing after I got my first period. I'm assuming this was to avoid the catastrophic reactions when the doctors would say a sixteen-year-old should most certainly have her period, no matter her muscular dystrophy or other issues. The one doctor who said this out loud, we never saw again.

When my mother was unconscious from Ambien, I went on a search for information about the outside world—what friends did together, what relationships looked like, how to kiss, how teenagers spent their day, what kids in classrooms did, and how teenagers spoke. I knew our new neighbor Aleah was probably a teenager, and I thought I was just a kid, but hormones were flooding me, and I became curious about boys.

If I was found out, I would be in big trouble. Not just for the laptop use, but for the "impure" thoughts. Punishments ranged from the physical to the emotional to the supernatural. I remember a trip to the store when my mother marched in and handpicked the "right" raw cow's tongue. She needed it for a recipe, but not the kind from a Barefoot Contessa cookbook, as my mother didn't eat meat. She was cooking up a spell.

Whenever I would compare our "normal" to how other people lived, my mother dissuaded my protest by reminding me that she and my grandmother had certain powers. Sometimes I still believe it, especially the part that I'll never be free. It's really easy to be brought back into line if you think your mother will go out back and mix a potion in a cauldron to punish you forever. Maybe she had watched *Snow White* too many times, with the mother casting her fair daughter out for the hunter's delight, jealous of her coming of age.

If I ever questioned our lifestyle, the gas reimbursements, why she kept telling doctors I wasn't old enough to have a period, why she would tell a lie to a friend, or why I couldn't have friends "my age," my mother would remind me of her witchcraft powers. A pencil would fall off the table, and she'd say she did it with her mind. The showerhead would drip water, and she'd claim it was the force of her energy. The little house on Volunteer Way could swallow me up whole if my mother just willed it to.

So my mother was not only my sole caretaker, without whom I could die for any reason at any time, she was like a god to me, with omniscient powers. If I wanted to sleep alone once in a while, she would say with indifference, "I hope nothing happens to you tonight." And then close the bedroom door. I became afraid of the dark real quick. Of course, this would result in my begging to sleep with her, waiting for her to have mercy on me. "You are my heart," she'd say while we snuggled away the adrenaline rush I felt from being alone in the dark.

Her emotions were a whip that snapped against my self-worth. I found solace and escape in drugs, especially after we began fighting a lot. Though I was prescribed pain medications once in a while for a dental issue or a minor surgery, my mother had frequent prescriptions for Vicodin and oxycodone. She had chronic kidney stones and chronic pain in her leg. I was well aware that those drugs had a calming effect on me, and once I began to question her and also push back as a teenager for more freedom and independence, our fighting really spun me out. I remember the first time I sought out the painkillers for no pain at all, and it was after Mama and I were yelling at each other for what seemed like over an hour. I just wanted to relax. So I popped one of her pills and exhaled.

The pills became a thrilling turbulence to my static air, a friend to depend on, a disturbance of my monotony. They also were the only things to numb my pain and rescue me from my loneliness. She knew I was taking them and didn't say a word. Well into my later teen years, when I began to question and rebel, I think she preferred I had my "secret" high because at least she knew something could control me when she couldn't. At the very least, the pills shut me up.

Soon one pill wasn't enough, so I'd double up, and then, high as kite, surf late at night on my laptop. Then I'd graduate to crushing the pills and inserting them in my feeding tube, which gave me an instant high. The only time Mama got really mad at me was when she needed the pills for her migraines and there weren't any left.

"The pharmacy won't refill these before it's time!" she yelled one afternoon. Caring only about my fix, I freaked out at the thought that the one crutch I actually needed was gone. I *needed* them to be refilled. She needed them to be refilled. So she dragged me to the police station with her and told the detective that she and I were robbed in the Walmart parking lot and the thugs ran off with her only bottle of pain meds. With the police report, she was able to justify a refill.

Being high uninhibited me. The pills gave me the nerve to comment in chat rooms in the middle of the night. I dressed up in wigs and showed off my cleavage in self-portraits. The pills provided a hopeful escape from my boredom, confusion, fear, and loneliness. They provided me with a fuzzy courage to find ways to explore my teenage curiosities and fulfill my foreign and tingly new needs.

I went from wishing for a daddy to fishing for a boyfriend.

EIGHT

Gris-Gris

A curse

It's so cliché, but by the time I was real-age nineteen, I couldn't turn off the need for a man, any man, in my life. I'd started a secret MySpace page and then a secret Facebook account.

Mama and I had seen an advertisement on TV for VisionCon, a pop culture convention held every year in Missouri. We went three years in a row, beginning in 2009. I waited for every spring to come just to dress up and do something fun with Mama.

So I began adding people from the convention to my online friends lists.

I received a Facebook message from Dan around March 2011. In his friend request, he reminded me that he was the "drunk guy" who bumped into my wheelchair at VisionCon the month before.

71

Dan was much older than me, in his thirties, and thought I was fifteen. I already exhibited "daddy issues," as I grew to have a mad crush on him.

Mama obviously didn't know I was spending months talking to Dan, exploring who I could be if allowed to be my own person. What color would my hair be if it were allowed to grow in? What kinds of restaurants would I like to eat at, if I were allowed to eat? What kinds of concerts would I go to, if I were allowed to listen to popular music? What kind of kisser would I be, if I were allowed to see Dan?

Dan was the first person I ever told that I could walk. I unburdened myself to him, telling him how my mother told stories to people, scolded me if she saw me accidentally move my legs, and how I was becoming increasingly worried about going to specialists. I was always high when talking to Dan, dreaming about moving away with him, being quirky and silly, always telling him jokes. One day while Mama and I were being put up at the American Cancer Society Hope Lodge in Kansas City while visiting doctors at Mercy Hospital, Dan and I communicated through phone calls on a government burner phone, one of three that Mama had. I hadn't done any rebelling yet, so Mama didn't have any reason not to trust me with one of the phones, plus she didn't think I had anyone to call or text anyway. So, she gave me the phone like you'd give an old cell phone to a child to play with as a toy.

Mama was in the kitchen and I was in the en suite bathroom, pacing around the tiled floor while talking to Dan, like any typical teenage girl swooning over a boyfriend. I had called to tell him I that I found my Medicaid card in my mother's wallet, and that despite her cover-up that it was a typo, I suspected I was older than my mom told me I was. The birth date on the card was four years earlier than I had known my birthday to be: July 27, 1991. I was horrified—but also relieved to think that I could actually be nineteen years old, not fifteen. I knew that my being of legal age could change a lot of things for me and Dan, so I put aside the thought that I was being held captive by an evil stepmother, and I focused on my fairy-tale godmother, granting my wish to be with my prince. Dan told me, "If this is true, you don't have to stay with her. You can start a new life."

Just as his words stirred my heart, Mama opened the door to the bathroom. Immediately, I hit the floor. "I'm sorry, I'm sorry, Mama," I said, covering my head with my hands. She grabbed the phone and heard a man's voice and hung up. Even behind closed doors, I was not ever to get out of my wheelchair, stand, or walk. I was in double jeopardy now. First, for walking; and second, for talking to a man.

She just stood there without saying a word, letting me beg for mercy.

"Get. In. Your. Chair. And now get to the van," she ordered, and then grabbed the phone off the floor.

Her calmness unsettled me. In the van, my stomach curled as I watched her eyes shift around the Kansas City streets.

"Mama, what's happening? Where are we going?"

She looked right through me. "You goddamn whore!" she said.

We rounded a corner and she pulled the minivan into an alleyway and threw the car into park. She turned to me, looked at my legs, and began punching them. She attacked every healthy, active muscle in my quads and thighs, like she was a boxer and I was a piece of meat hanging in a freezer locker. I didn't know you could bleed without cutting the skin. Redness began to rise to the surface and create little blood clots, which later formed blood blisters.

She had never closed-fist punched me before. I sobbed so hard, I couldn't catch my breath. "I'm sorry, Mama, please stop." She looked checked out, and I knew she couldn't hear me above her own disgusted yelling: "What did you tell him?" "Where did you meet him? Who is he?" "I leave for a moment and this is what you do?"

She was getting winded, but each question was followed by a blow to my legs. "How much did you tell him?"

"I didn't tell him anything, Mama."

"Liar! Fucking cunt!"

Then she grabbed my face with one hand and squeezed my cheeks together, forcing my lips to pucker. The tips of her fingernails dug into my skin. She looked me square in the eyes.

"I hate you," she said.

My fear of being under her thumb forever went from a feeling to an urgent fact. She thought she had her ultimate control of me locked in, but I had veered outside her radius, causing her to lose sight of me. She declared a dogfight, where her new combat maneuver was to gain positional control over me. Punch after punch, the shiny bruises on my legs were marks of the true colors of her soul—black and blue.

Mama read my text messages and then hastily dialed Dan's number. She didn't introduce herself when he answered. "You know she's only fifteen," she barked. "If you contact her again, I'll call the cops."

Dan and I turned down the heat after that, but only for a couple of weeks. When I sensed her cloud of anger evaporating, I began talking on the phone to Dan again, this time to unload all the suspicions I had about my medical history. It was a relief to confide in someone. He showed me attention and let me speak. I thought it was possible for him to take me out of my captive existence. He told me he had a farm in Arkansas, that we could run away there, and he'd hide me. I told him I didn't think I had cancer, and that I could walk, and I was so confused. *Who am I? Who is she? And why is she doing this?*

"You are technically an adult," Dan said. "You can start a new life."

I look back on my first attempt to run away with Dan as the biological and natural urge brought on by growing up, individualizing. Puberty was a taboo subject, but just the same, along with the metamorphosis of my body, my developing prefrontal cortex was taking me for a joyride. As hard as Mama tried to conceal the changes, she was powerless over the deluge of hormones and the critical thinking that became a voice in my head. Just because I couldn't see a woman in the mirror doesn't mean my brain wasn't fighting hard as hell to become one. I didn't understand this at the time, but I believe it was the intense power of nature that guided my compulsion to separate from her. We all have to grow up. Turns out mothers can't fight Mother Nature.

At around two o'clock in the morning of Good Friday, April 22, Dan texted Mama's phone, which I had hidden in my dresser drawer on my side of the bed. "I'm in the hospital," the text said. "I got beat up real bad. I'd like you to be with me." So I grabbed the phone, and my government phone, which had run out of minutes, and stuffed them inside a backpack full of girl-woman confusion. I had to go to him. I packed up a *Lilo & Stitch* movie, my baby bottle and change of nipples, a pair of stolen jeans, and stolen lingerie. As I stole Mama's cash and oxy stash, I was scared as hell. I threw on a pair of oversized jeans, since I didn't know my size; I had stolen them a few weeks before in preparation for running away. The jeans felt scratchy at first; it was the first time I wore anything "fashionable." I put on a stolen black tank top, over a red bra that was two sizes too big, and a beach-wave blonde wig. I scribbled a note in the darkness of the kitchen, left it on the seat of my wheel-chair, and slipped out the back door:

Dear Mother,

I know I can walk. I don't think I have cancer. I don't feel sick. I know that I am really nineteen. I want to live my own life as an independent woman. I love you. It is just time for me to spread my wings and fly. I am going up to St. Louis.

I love you,

Your grown-up daughter

Walking up the street, I felt out of breath because I wasn't used to carrying the weight of my own body. In the middle of the night, I walked to the subdivision of houses across the street, knocked on a stranger's door, and asked for a ride to see my boyfriend in the hospital.

When I arrived at the hospital emergency room, I texted Dan. I had been in this same ER, too many times to count, with my mom. My adrenaline was pumping, and I just wanted to lie as low as possible for fear I'd be recognized. I stayed with Dan until he was released, and we caught a ride home with his cousin.

Dan was couch surfing at a friend's house, so his cousin took us back there. When we arrived, I was tentative with Dan. Looking at the bongs and the bugs all around the apartment, I was disheartened that I hadn't escaped to the perfect picture I had drawn in my mind.

"Come lay with me," Dan said, as he showed me to the spare room, where he lay down on the mattress. I joined him, my hand covering my feeding tube, a gaping symbol of how starved I was. I lay with Dan, pecked him on the cheek, fidgeting my body so he wouldn't feel the tube and willing myself to fit into him like a human jigsaw.

"When will we leave tomorrow?" I asked him, trusting he had handled the logistics.

That's when he told me he couldn't leave the state. He was on parole.

I didn't know what parole was and began to cry. I was partly let down, partly scared for what this would mean for me. Dan had been in jail? I risked so much by leaving Mama and now I was with someone who couldn't take care of me. I couldn't go back to her house, especially not after I lied, stole, and ran away. But how could I go with him?

I spoke with Dan in a panic. I was sandwiched between two hopeless options. "I'll find work in St. Louis," Dan said, trying to reassure me.

Then Dan's friend knocked on the bedroom door and leaned against the doorframe.

"Hey, what's your name?" he asked, with a knowing look on his face.

"Gypsy?" I answered, instantly regretful of telling the truth.

"Your mother's here."

It happened so fast—but in slow motion. My brain couldn't quite catch up to what was happening. It was six or seven in the morning, and she had tracked me down, with the help of some convention friends who knew Dan. I stood up from the bed. She looked at my legs with the same disdain she had in the alleyway.

"Where's the money?" Mama asked, eyeballing Dan. "Gypsy, talk to me on the porch."

I don't know what Dan or his friends were thinking, but like a puppy dog, I followed her to the porch.

"Get in the van," she said, with a hint of understanding. "We'll talk about this."

"No, Mama. I know that I'm nineteen years old and I can be with him if I want to."

She didn't react or try to gaslight me. Instead, she bargained, as if I had attained some equality and control of my destiny. "If you come back with me, I will let you see him," Mama said.

"Promise?" I think I believed her out of hope that she was seeing me as the person I was growing into, somehow magically becoming aware of my awareness.

"Yes. Go get your stuff and we'll go home."

She threatened Dan one more time, and later told all our mutual acquaintances that he was a pedophile. I never heard from him again.

When we got home, Mama tore through my backpack. Upon seeing the lingerie, she made me take a pregnancy test. "You whore! If you're pregnant," she scowled, "you are getting an abortion." Provocative words from a woman who didn't utter the word "period" to me my entire life. It was as if the smokescreen had lifted for a second, and she and I dropped the pretenses. She was talking to a nineteen-year-old, and we both knew it.

I went into the bathroom and looked in the mirror, something Mama told me I should never do on Good Friday. "You will see Jesus dying on the cross, if you look at yourself. Avoid the mirror on Good Friday," she used to say.

She printed a picture of Dan from his Facebook page and then smashed my laptop and my TracFone. She took a mason jar and shoved a picture of me and the picture of Dan into it, with a cow's tongue—the tongue was to represent silencing me. She dropped a piece of toilet paper that had some of my period blood in the jar and buried it in the backyard, not far from the shed. I observed her bizarre behavior, like an outsider, detached and confused. She chanted over me, something like "By God, Gypsy-Rose will never find true love. Gypsy-Rose will never find happiness."

All I heard was *Gypsy will never be free.*

Her spell came true, because the next thing I knew, she made me go back into the house, handcuffed me to a dog leash, and connected the leash to her. "Please, I'm sorry. I'll be good, Mama," was my refrain. She placed bells on the doors and reinforced the black garbage bags taped to every window in the house. I was trapped. If she fell asleep, I couldn't move without waking her up. I was at her mercy for everything—to go to the bathroom, for food, for everything. As punishment, she would not feed me every day, just a little bit of broth every other day. I would frequently get hunger pains. She was right beside me and would eat whatever she wanted. She kept a knife by her bedside table, which she said was for protection if I attempted to run away or do anything to leave.

This went on for two weeks. Any love we had for each other was replaced by a mistrust that filled the house like a pressure cooker. The superficiality of our relationship had unraveled. Nobody came looking for either of us. Mama had made sure to establish strict boundaries that people knew not to cross. People knew well enough not to question her reclusive moods, mere cycles of a psyche that nobody, especially me, understood.

Mama wouldn't talk to me. Even when it came time to administer my medicines, she gave me the silent treatment. We knew the drill, so words were not required. For two weeks, she just kept me chained to the bedpost or to her body, and the extreme closeness to her skin made me feel thousands of miles apart from her. When I was little, I loved the feel of her skin on mine. Nothing made me feel safe and loved like sleeping next to her, the warmth radiating from her body, blanketing me. Now, the warmth was replaced by electricity, fencing me in. How long will I be locked in here? Sooner or later, we'd need to go to a doctor or run an errand. She did leave me for short periods of time to go to a homeowners' association meeting or to pick up something to eat. I'd be so afraid that a fire would suddenly start, and the firefighters would find me burnt to a crisp, tied to the bed.

I talked to nobody for two weeks, nobody, except for God.

It had been a while since I'd prayed. I used to have formal prayer time at church every Sunday. When it came to churches, we bounced around a lot. Like how a young person explores her identity, Mama tried on churches for size. After we left Golden Meadows and distanced ourselves from the Pitres, I think Mama went exploring for a religion that was independent of what she experienced growing up Catholic, yet still familiar. We went to several different Christian churches when we moved near New Orleans, and then stayed nondenominational, even going to some really wonky churches in odd locations, like strip malls or a random house on a residential street.

I prayed to God to shield me from the mason jar spell Mama had cast on me, but I also apologized to him for not being in touch for such a long time. I examined my Communion portrait that hung from the living room wall, my eight-year-old hands pressed together in prayer, my small frame cloaked in a miniature wedding dress for God. Did I still know that little girl, so full of hope and faith and belief and blind trust? All of which now had vanished, along with the illusion that my mother loved me and wanted me safe. "God, please tell Mama to forgive me. I will be good. Make me clean."

He must have heard me. Because on the fourteenth day, she woke me up by unlocking the handcuffs and untethering me from the leash. The knife, however, would remain on the nightstand.

NINE

Allons

Let's go.

Maybe Mama really had magic powers, because in the months leading up to my second escape attempt in 2012, I knew by the way she increased her surveillance of me that she sensed I was up to something. I couldn't even go to the bathroom without asking permission. It took months to regain Mama's trust after she unleashed me from the bedpost. If I had been allowed to walk, it would've been on eggshells, as I did everything in my power not to upset her. I took my medicine and wore my oxygen at night, the ruse now an open flesh wound, but still ongoing. It was our normal, and I needed it back, so at least she'd take the bell off the back door.

What kept me going was the hope of an escape, and that hope was crammed in a backpack hidden behind the couch. That, and the painkillers. I don't know if it was my nervous energy, but she was tipped off and went on one of her maniacal searches of the house. She ransacked my bedroom, not exactly knowing what she was looking for, but likely thinking she'd know it when she saw it. I followed her in my wheelchair, crying, "What are you doing? What are you looking for? What did I do?"

After she dumped out all my drawers, she continued to the living room. I slickly maneuvered my wheelchair to block the couch cushion—I was a human compass arrow that led the pirate right to its booty.

"Move out of the way," my mother said, her eyes darting.

I knew I couldn't deny the evidence.

"Can't you just let me leave—let me go?" I pleaded, looking past her to the kitchen table where her favorite talisman—an old-fashioned Chinese dagger—lay.

"Not this again, Gypsy. I thought we moved past this."

She sounded like I was begging her to let me go to the mall or to even date Dan, who wanted nothing to do with me after she told everyone that he was a pervert and a child molester.

"I won't bother you, and you'll never see me again," I said, saying the reverse of what she wanted to hear.

Rushing to the kitchen table, I swiped the dagger and grabbed a .22-caliber BB gun she'd picked up at Walmart. I thought if I aimed the gun at her, she'd back off. Out of fear, I pulled the trigger and offloaded ten BBs at her, creating tiny slits in her flesh.

"You shot me!"

She backed her way into the bathroom. Double fisted with weaponry, I followed her until I was wedged in the doorway.

"Give me my bag. I want to go." I came at her with the gun, now empty, and just held the dagger up while she sat on the toilet. We were at a standoff.

"Why can't I be like other kids?" This surge of heat released from the top of my head. I could feel my arms quivering and my voice trembling. I didn't know frustration could feel this way, like you want to twist your own head off and throw it at someone. "Why do you shave my head? Why can't I be like Aleah? Why is my life this way?"

All the questions ... I was mad about Dan, and about the dog's leash, and about the cow's tongue. The loneliness, the shame, the period pull-up diapers, the pills that made me drowsy, the surgeries. I wanted a dad; I wanted a friend; I wanted to laugh; I wanted to listen to the Backstreet Boys.

"I love you," she said, pressing her fingers against her bleeding flesh wounds. "You are my heart, and I can't live without my heart."

And then I asked the question that had been the source of so much frustration: "Why can't you let me go?"

"Because I need you."

I put the dagger down but held on to the empty gun.

"Please stay," she begged.

I released all that pent-up anger. I felt a relief. Then remorse. I saw her flesh wounds, and I felt sorry and apologetic that it had escalated to this. I had forgotten that she said she hated me in the alley. All that echoed in my mind now was "I love you."

We sat on the bed together while she tended to her leg with peroxide and Band-Aids. I couldn't stop crying.

The day went by with my quiet sobs. There was hardly anything said. She didn't hit me or tie me up again. I think she was afraid of me. I think she hadn't realized Baby could be violent. Honey and Baby were equals now. I was scared shitless of her, and she was scared shitless of me. Another dogfight, this time nose to nose.

The whole time, I never got up from the wheelchair. But from here on, Mama and I were speaking different languages.

TEN

Meeting Nick

I met Nick on christiandatingforfree.com on October 12, 2012. Creating my profile allowed me the freedom to create something real and let go of my false persona. I dressed the way I thought I would look if I had grown up normal. The picture I posted was me wearing a brown wig, because my hair would've been brown if my mother hadn't shaved it off. I wore a prom dress that my mother bought on clearance from JCPenney after prom season ended. Lying across my couch, I posed with a rose. I felt beautiful in my body. I liked having breasts and hips. Maybe I was on the way to finding myself, exploring myself.

But that came to a screeching halt when I got matched with a boy named Nick who "winked" at me.

He must've liked my profile description, which said basically: "I'm a very happy, bubbly girl interested in sci-fi and fantasy. I am a virgin and am waiting to commit myself to my husband."

Innocently, I added my love for animals and being outside— even though my time in nature was contained to brief visits to my backyard, marveling at butterflies and slugs. When I was surfing the internet, I was a butterfly. Nick said he wanted this butterfly to be his girlfriend, and it was the first time I experienced the feeling of pride. Someone wanted me for me. I wanted love and attention that had nothing to do with pity, so I made the videos he requested and directed. The more he praised me for a "good job," after sucking on a dildo he had ordered from Japan, the more I believed he loved me. Of course, when I would do the videos "wrong," e.g., forgetting to call him "master" or not being a dirty enough girl, he'd threaten to pull that love away. I was familiar with the carrot-and-stick game. My mother loved me when I was sick and took her love back when I wasn't. In order to be accepted and loved, I needed to meet the expectations of others.

Nick exposed me to a lot of sexually perverse things and ideas, but ten years later, knowing now what I know about sex, he taught me all wrong. From what I've read, he didn't have an accurate idea of BDSM (bondage, discipline, submission, and masochism), and he made it up as we went along.

The BDSM stuff made me cringe, and after a while it demoralized me. I felt uncomfortable in the role of his submissive and winced when he verbally degraded me. But Nick would balance that out with an intricate fantasy world containing realms of good versus evil, which reminded me of the sci-fi conventions and the stories and movies I enjoyed and needed to believe in.

I was vulnerable to Nick—the only adult in my life who knew that I could walk, that I didn't have labored breathing at bedtime, that I wasn't mentally disabled, that the scars on both sides of my neck were from an unnecessary surgery, that I'd be under the knife again soon enough. I took off one mask of Gypsy-Rose, replacing it with another mask of Gypsy-Rose. Telling the truth felt like releasing a butterfly from a net—only for it to fly right into the mud.

We both lived in a fantasy world, where the innocence of imagination dies and resurrects into a world ruled by the improbable and the impossible. Nick lived in the realm of the improbable. In our elaborate conversations, he'd command his many minions and gargoyles to swoop me out of my princess room and into a dimension in which I was queen. His queen.

Nick's storytelling captivated me. Precise and colorful, detailed and well crafted, if he hadn't included the perversion and the savage and depraved violence, he could've turned his stories into novels and sold millions of copies. I could feel the grooves of the stone walls of his castle and the smoothness of the horns of the cerapters circling the labyrinth. Proper names for his creations rolled off his tongue, suspending my belief in glorious ways. Night after night, I drank from his chalice of escape. Nick's realm held mystical beasts, evil spells, and poison potions—the upside-down version of my reality.

Like Earth's continents, Nick's fantasy world contained several lands separated by serpent-filled seas. Nick's evil twin brother lived in one realm, and he vowed to build a portal to the human world, where he would murder those in Nick's wake; in particular, me. Thank goodness for his medallion, his prized possession, which magically transported Nick out of this brother's realm and into his secret realm of safety, which was also Nick's kingdom. Here he was king and lived amongst twelve alien soulmates of different species. I was the only human soulmate, his queen . . . but not without a duty. And if I didn't fulfill it, I'd be cast out forever, losing the one king who would ever love me.

This kingdom is where Victor, the three-thousand-year-old vampire, lived. It was also home to the Dark One. These villains did not drink blood; they thirsted, however, for rape and murder of women, and not always in that order. Nick also had such a thirst for necrophilia, as he shared his fantasy of first murdering and then raping his ex-girlfriend, after which he'd meticulously carve her skin with a knife to brand her with labels, like "whore," "bitch," and "slut."

In Nick's realm, king and queen did not sit side by side, but as dominant and submissive, the queen being ruled over in all aspects. And it wasn't just sex. I'd only speak when told I could speak. I'd be chastised for laughing at something funny because I hadn't yet been permitted. I could not make advances or ask questions without a code word. I role-played with four different personas: "Demona," who was a half-werewolf, half-human girl; "Kitty," who was childlike; "Candy" embraced more of my "slutty side"; and "Ruby" was the "evil one."

Our laptop cameras became a portal between his realm and mine, transporting us both into our respective roles, me dressing in costume, taking orders, speaking in the language of the realm, and addressing Nick as "Master."

He would protect me from anyone, yes, even his evil twin brother, but only if I was a good girl and did what I was told. You have to understand: I thought my having a boyfriend would bring me one step closer to being a real teenager, like my neighbor Aleah and her friends. I thought that having a Facebook profile and liking and sharing things was going to ultimately initiate me into a culture club filled with peers and people watching and an actual community, of which I was an active participant. If I couldn't physically reach out and touch that world, I'd bring the world closer to touch me.

When Nick ordered me to touch myself, I thought it was his way of teleporting his touch to me, my hand a mere lever he was controlling with a joystick from his dark kingdom in a faraway land called Wisconsin. Before I met Nick, my profile picture was of me in a yellow ruffled sundress, a floppy hat, holding a teddy bear. Where my mother defeminized me, by putting a razor on my vagina, Nick told me I'd be a woman if he carved me up with a knife. Where my mother humiliated my femininity by binding my breasts, Nick ordered me to humiliate myself by slathering them with barbeque sauce or peanut butter. I was a mechanical doll, taking instructions and acting them out, without pleasure or pain. I just was. Because I believed I was learning what love is. It is someone caring enough about you to dominate you; it is caring enough about someone to fulfill all his commands.

The validation I'd receive from Nick kept me compliant and submissive. In order to be accepted, I needed to keep him happy. I had no other suitors, no other reference point. I was alone, and I wanted my aloneness to be cured, to treat it because it was the one true disease I actually had. Here is a guy who is into this odd stuff, okay, but how bad can it be? Maybe guys his age explore sexually in this way? How would I know or not know? I just wanted to be accepted, and I thought I'd do anything he wanted to stay in his life, even if that life was in a world of his own making. I had already lived in a world of someone else's making. At least in his I was a woman.

"I'm so proud of you," he said, after I sent him my "initiation" video, which formally defined our roles in the BDSM relationship. At the end of the video I had to say, "Please consider me as your submissive." As elaborate as the details of his fantasy realms, Nick would send me scripts to act out, direct my dialogue and costuming, and demand unusual sexual behaviors with phallic objects while contorting my body so my female parts were exposed like parts under the hood of a rusty old car.

The acting felt natural. During the day I was a hairless prepubescent paraplegic child, squeaky-voiced, running through scripts that prompted doctors to poke and prod me. At night, I was running through scripts begging for the mercy of my master, as I poked and prodded myself. Day or night, mother or master, my identity was created in the image of a two-headed monster, a monster whose fetish was to feast on my dignity.

Nick pulled BDSM through like a thread in his fantasy world stories. There was no separation between the realms and our dominant and submissive acts. Whatever we would be doing or saying as dominant and submissive was all in service of his kingdom or the realm, where the Dark One, where Victor, and where Nick's evil twin were all out to get me, to pillage me and make me scream in horror, and degrade my womanhood with each painful thrust of their daggers.

He wanted me to denigrate myself with a nine-inch dildo he had mail ordered from Japan. I remember him ordering me to stalk the mailman, because something was coming for me. I did intercept the unmarked package, and the thought of shoving the object up me made me queasy. Bad girl that I was, I told my master NO when he told me to put it in all three of my holes. So, I just sucked on it for him, taking out my dentures to try to ease the gag reflex so I wouldn't vomit in my mouth. He called me names: "whore, cunt, bitch." All the while my tongue painted the plastic—up, down, all around. The feeling of confused shame was familiar as I heard my grandfather's voice in my head. Minutes lasted between sounds of my swallowing and smacking, until finally Nick ordered me to stop.

I overlooked the malevolence and the kink in order to build something that wasn't there—a life with Nick. "If I were free, what would it be like to live together?" I'd ask him, unaware that he was engaged in video relationships with at least three other women. It wasn't just about having Nick control my life, I wanted to imagine our romance coming to life in my realm, the real world. What would it be like to be king and queen? I waited for Nick's answers with bated breath, but his answers were all about being his sex slave and fighting the forces of the Dark One.

I agreed to the "terms" of Nick's dominance over me. In his mind, this meant we were married. "I own you now" would become his refrain. He said that one day soon, he'd take my virginity from me. Because that's what dominants do. I invested a lot of time and energy in capturing his acceptance and what I thought was love, while he captured my mind. He would say things like, "I'm so proud of you," if I rubbed the right amount of barbeque sauce or ketchup on my naked body in a bathtub. "You have so much potential, Gypsy," he'd say. If I was good at humiliating myself for his pleasure, he'd tell me he loved me and he believed in me. Other times, he'd say I needed bigger boobs or I wasn't dirty or nasty enough.

Nick introduced the violence, the murders, the blood, the carvings, the brutal rape fantasies, and I was so afraid of losing his validation. I ignored his ex-girlfriend's Facebook message warning that he was controlling and "not all there."

"What girl wants to see her ex happy?" Nick rationalized, when I told him his ex messaged me. It wasn't until he told me that upon our daughter's thirteenth birthday, he would take her virginity that I thought he crossed the creepy line. I broke up with him, but like a good submissive, I accepted his apologies and returned to our status quo, the same way I accepted my mother's non-apologies.

The endgame was to live a life together and to finally be together, and the ideas of how I wanted to be treated and how he wanted to treat me were different. We'd argue a lot about this. "Why can't we have a normal life?" I'd say, my begging indirectly feeding into his dominance. "Like the people on *Malcolm in the Middle*? Why can't we have that family?"

He didn't want an American sitcom kind of life. "I'm not that kind of person," he responded, firm on the fact he wouldn't change, that people don't change. "You must not really love me if you want to change me."

We would go back and forth on the matter of shifting our relationship from dominant and submissive to an American sitcom kind of life. We'd threaten breaking up with each other, which triggered an anxiety of being abandoned, which is something I still grapple with today. Our fights would shine a light on my feelings of unworthiness, which only made me sabotage the relationship even more. He'd do the same, and he'd continue his threats to leave me, and the cycle would continue. Finally, I'd beg him not to leave me and cave in to do whatever he wanted me to do.

ELEVEN

The Movie Theater

Nick and I wanted to be together, and we both wanted me out of my mother's grip. He could protect me by taking me away, by moving me to Wisconsin with him, and by sharing a life with me. So we talked about the options we could exercise to make that happen, as we tried to manipulate the mangled parts of my life into a more pleasant shape.

We didn't have a master plan. It wasn't anything like that, like planning a jewelry heist, with several plots or run-throughs. I had been a hopeless, sheltered girl who had found hope in Nick and then lost that hope all over again, when my mother's physical abuse reinforced the electric fence that she had activated after the Dan debacle. It wasn't one discussion like, "Okay, how do we get rid of your mom?" They were gradual conversations that were baked into an elaborate fantasy world Nick created. He shared with me that he got sexually aroused when he fantasized about murdering and then raping his ex-girlfriend, but our plot was more reminiscent of a soap opera.

"I got it!" I said to Nick, brainstorming an idea for one option. "You come visit me in the middle of the night, and when Mama's asleep, I'll wheel down the wheelchair ramp and you and I will sneak to the backyard. We'll have sex and you will get me pregnant, and then Mama will have to let me be with you. As the father, she will have to accept you."

I shoplifted prenatal pills and a pregnancy test and posted it on my secret Facebook page, where I was friends with Nick's mom. She called Nick: "What is Gypsy doing?" Okay, that's not a good plan.

Nick said his mother was not pleased and warned him not to get me pregnant. It is eerie how this story is almost exactly the same as when Grandma Sharon warned my dad against Mama trying to get pregnant because of a library book.

I'm not sure why I thought Mama would be on board with a pregnancy. When she accused me of having sex with Dan, even though I swore up and down nothing happened, she said she'd make me have an abortion if I was pregnant. Nick was right—pregnancy wouldn't work.

I really had to dig in to try to understand what my mother's big issue about me dating was. Her control and abuse had moved outside the realm of my health and was more preoccupied with my social interactions, especially romantic ones, which my maturing body and mind naturally craved. Was she afraid of being abandoned by me? That I'd meet a man, make a family, and forget all about her? Was it that she would be jealous or feel left out of my life in some way? My thought process was so desperate. I thought if I could figure out a way to placate her emotional needs, there would be a way for me to create a win-win situation, one in which I was happy with Nick and my mother could feel like an active participant in my life.

I continued brainstorming with Nick, coming up with what I thought was the best idea yet. "What if we accidentally meet up and pretend we just met, and Mama would see that we really like each other and let us date?"

"Like pretend we are strangers who bump into each other, like love at first sight?" he asked.

"Exactly. Mama and I go to the movies a lot, so maybe you can come down when we see the new *Cinderella* movie, and then you are just there in the lobby and we accidentally meet, like bump into each other."

This meet-cute idea made sense to me at the time. Mama wanted to be a part of my life and wouldn't let go, so what if I baked her into the origin story? "The first time Nick and I met, Mama was there," I would say at our wedding, with Mama by my side, happily taking credit for my happiness.

I was delusional to think Mama would find peace in knowing she was a part of us and not feel alienated or threatened in any way. But I figured our love story would be her story as much as it was mine. She could own it. We shared everything, after all, so this had to be the answer. I had to share my experience with Nick with her to appeal to her ego, so she wouldn't feel excluded—or worse, replaced. At least that's what I thought she needed in order to let me date him. I was trying to get her approval in my life in any way, just so Nick could somehow be integrated. It was when she felt excluded, or she felt I was "leaving her," that she'd unleash her wrath.

Nick made an addition to our meet-cute plan. "I will take your virginity at the movie theater," he said, with lust in his voice. "And you will be mine forever. I will own you."

At this point, I wanted to give him my virginity, mostly because I wanted that part over with. I thought this was my one and only chance, especially as I was finally getting to be with Nick in real life. *This is something we have to do now,* I thought. We promised we would figure out a way for us to meet in the bathroom during the movie.

So on March 12, 2015, I dressed up in a Cinderella costume dress and tiara to accompany Mama to the live-action film version of *Cinderella.* We were regulars at the movie theater in Springfield and were greeted by the staff with the usual enthusiasm they'd shown for us ever since we moved to town. It was like any other day, except I had cramps from being on my period. I double dosed on oxy to help with the cramps. My diaper felt particularly sticky against the flammable polyester material of my princess dress. The damn diaper was riding up me, and I felt like I already needed to change. I looked around eagerly, wishing I didn't feel so gross, because my Prince Charming was literally going to appear, as planned, any second. I smiled and wheeled slowly through the lobby. In seconds my life would change forever.

And as promised, Nick appeared. He was a terrible actor, as he awkwardly came over and said hello to me. Looking back now, I could see how transparent the whole scene was, and my mother didn't buy any of it. I wanted to sit with Nick, and she demanded I stay with her. She thought he was creepy. Why is there this single adult man at a kids' movie? She had already figured Dan to be a pedophile, and considering both our histories with Claude, I don't think Mama's concern about Nick was far off.

I told her I was going to the bathroom. She let me go alone. Looking back now, I don't know why she did. Was it a trap? Did she want to give me enough rope to hang myself? If she didn't let me go, she wouldn't have been able to punish me. Or did she really let her guard down? After Dan, I don't think that was possible.

Prepared to be transformed by my first sexual encounter, I wheeled into the men's bathroom and Nick fell in line, following me into the wheelchair-accessible stall. If my mother came looking for me, I knew she wouldn't go into the men's room.

It was exciting. After almost a year of a virtual relationship, to be in the flesh together felt like a dream. We kissed awkwardly, not too slow because we knew we had to be quick. As his hands glided down and underneath my princess dress, I winced when his hand froze. I sensed his brain trying to register what his fingers were feeling as he inched them down the front of not sexy underwear but a diaper. And the moisture he felt was not due to the heat he was producing inside me but blood.

Nick went limp. He saw my diaper and the blood, and without the need for my explanation, he put two and two together. I tried to touch him to help him regain an erection, but there was nothing I could do to help him unsee a grown woman bleeding into a diaper. In the name of his owning me, Nick pressed his softness against me and tried to stuff himself inside, unable to penetrate me with his power.

I wheeled out of the stall, technically still a virgin.

Nick said we were married now, because what we just did, according to him, was sex.

The credits began to roll when Mama found me where I had been seated with Nick, and she looked blankly at me. Nick tried to make small talk, but she just walked out of the theater and then out of the front doors of the IMAX building.

"I better go," I said to Nick, a nervousness rising within me. He escorted me to the front doors and told me he'd call me when he got on the bus back to Wisconsin. Nick's mother had bought him the bus ticket, since he didn't work. He told me he used to have a job being the guy who held up the Little Caesars sign on the major roads, but that didn't work out. He spent a lot of time hanging out in the McDonald's that was within walking distance of his house, since they had Wi-Fi there. I didn't know then that Nick had been arrested for disorderly conduct, for masturbating to porn at the McDonald's. That was something that came out in the discovery process after our arrests. To be honest, even if he had told me, it probably wouldn't have stopped me from dating him.

Mama was not a fast walker, but on this day she was way ahead of me, already in the parking lot. I was spinning the wheels of my chair calling her name: "Mama, wait for me." She just proceeded to get into the van, pretending not to hear me, dismissing me completely. I knew she wouldn't leave me there. It would be too visible, too high profile. I met her at the van, transferred myself into the passenger seat, while without words, she folded up my chair, opened the back van door, and took some of her anger out on the wheelchair, flinging it inside.

"What were you thinking?" she said. I could tell she was seething because she was sighing to catch air, her breathing erratic and heavy. "Are you trying to kill me? You know I'm not well, Gypsy. I swear if I die, it will be you who killed me. You already tried to shoot me once."

All I could think of as she spoke so hatefully to me was that I wanted to get high.

"I didn't purposely try to kill you with BBs, Mama; I was trying to leave."

Any hope I had of being with Nick had been sucked out of me, along with my naivete. No plans could save me now. I didn't know what my fate would be with Nick being far away again and Mama more pissed off than ever. I closed my eyes and tried to calm myself with the thought of crushing Mama's oxy and injecting the pain-killing powder right into my feeding tube. Instant relief.

When we got back home, she took the handles of my wheelchair, signaling that she would be pushing me to my destination. Her cadence was pointed and determined as she marched me not up the wheelchair ramp to the front door but around the house and into the backyard.

"Mama, what's going on? I'm sorry, Mama. I'm sorry. I'll be good."

"Save it," she said. "You're a liar and you take me for a fool? You think you're just going to run off with this boy now? Whore. Fool me once . . ."

She walked us past the bald patch in the grass, where the cursed mason jar was buried, and brought me to the shed. When we were first given the Habitat for Humanity house, the program workers found out that I wished for a playhouse. So they painted the shed the same pink color as our house and made it look like a miniature version, a playhouse just for Gypsy.

Except I never went out there. For one thing, my mother never let me outside. There was never a moment during the day when Mama would ever say, "Let's get outside and get some sun on our face." Never. Second, I am afraid of bugs, and bugs were everywhere in the shed. The shed might have looked like a mini house, but the inside floor was made of dirt, where slugs and fire ants, and worse—spiders—lived.

As dusk blanketed the sky, the temperature dipped, and I was officially freaked out. I asked her cautiously, as if walking through a minefield, "Mama? What are we doing?"

"You can't be trusted," she said, her mind well made up. "Get in."

"No, stop, Mama!" My sobs failed to penetrate, bring her back to this world. She was somewhere else now, riding a wave of hatred and jealousy, fear and recklessness.

She pushed me into the shed. "Get out of the chair," she said. Even alone in the dark out back, where nobody would think to look for us, I transferred myself out of the chair as if my legs really didn't work. I placed myself on the ground, among the big black garbage bags full of shoplifted garments, tears spilling onto the dirt.

My stomach turns over when I play this moment back in my mind. I could've used the chair to bust right past her. She clearly didn't want to leave me alone in the shed with my wheelchair, in case I'd use it as a tool to break down the door. But I wonder if I would've done that at all. I look back at that little girl whose mind had been bent by a lifetime of indoctrination and see she wouldn't have fought back. Or maybe I was just too close to the cursed mason jar, where the spell still held power: *Gypsy will never be happy. She will never be free.*

She took an about-face and walked out, slamming the shed door behind her.

"Mama! Don't just leave me here, Mama! The spiders!"

The angry clanks of the padlock were her only response.

I was hungry, thirsty, freezing, scared, and the most desperate I had ever felt. And her pills were all the way back in the house.

Did Nick get on the bus okay? Is he asleep on the back of a comfortable coach bus, his head held up by the window? Was he a window or an aisle person? There was so much I didn't know about him that now I'd never find out. I tried to focus on Nick to keep my fear of the spiders at bay. *If I fall asleep, will they crawl in my ears and up my nose? Without my CPAP machine, will they creep into my mouth and lay eggs?* I had to stay awake and keep watch for Mama. Maybe she would miss me, alone in her bed, and come get me? I tried to send her telepathic messages. She always said we were connected in a special way, plus she had powers. *Come get me. Come get me. Come get me.*

After ripping open one of the bags to find warm clothes, I finally fell asleep. My telepathic messages worked, but not in the way I expected.

I had a dream in which Dad and Kristy were cooking in the kitchen of the little blue house. I was my age, but my body was childlike. I sat on the floor teasing my two cats with feather toys, but they turned into my brother and sister, Dylan and Mia. I was so happy but so mad at them at the same time. Happy because I was no longer alone, but mad because my dad had left me for them. Then suddenly, I'm at a police station with these really nice people wrapping blankets around me. Kristy and Dad were there talking to a detective. Kristy was crying, even though she looked happy.

The detective and the nice people with blankets met with all of us in a room. They were introducing me to Kristy and Dad because, in my dream, I didn't know them, even though I did. It's hard to explain.

"Gypsy, do you know where you are?" the detective asked.

"Where's Mama?" I asked, scanning the room of adults who looked at me like I was about to break.

They proceeded to tell me that Kristy and Dad had been looking for me all my life.

"Gypsy, we have to let you know that Dee Dee is not your real mother. Kristy is."

The police station transformed into an open park. Now, I was skipping around Disney World. My long, curly hair danced around my waist as I held the hands of Kristy and Dad, flanked by them. I felt a strong sense of relief that my life was not what it seemed— and finally someone did come get me.

When I woke up, I was disoriented. I looked around the shed and could see some sunlight peeking in. My fingers and toes were numb, and I must have slept hard because I had drool on my cheek. She had left me there all night, overnight, alone and scared. Depression drenched me, as I reconciled the fact that my dream wasn't real, that the pure joy I felt being reunited with my real family was as fictional as the life I lived with my mother.

Mama didn't come to let me out of the shed until about noon. She wasn't an early riser by habit, so why would she make a concession on this day? When she opened the door, her body language exuded the power of a victor over her spoils. I thought that upon seeing her, I'd be more afraid, or angry, or despondent. But I felt nothing, like all my emotions had been zapped out of me in a sterile shock-treatment room.

"Back to the house," she said, her hands gripping the portable wheelchair.

I transferred myself from the ground to the chair, and she wheeled me back to the house. We had an appointment with the ENT we couldn't miss.

TWELVE

Intermission: Recovering My Medical Records

Disclosure will bring closure. That's what I thought whenever I imagined the day when I would finally have all my medical records in my hands. And that day arrived in 2024, about three weeks after my release from Chillicothe Correctional Center. All the secret facts about my medical history were sprawled out on my living room floor in the apartment my husband Ryan and I moved into. I decided I'd really dive in once Ryan went back to work after the long holiday break. Sending him off to the school where he teaches somehow makes me feel like a wife, like we are really married. I think it's because him leaving also implies he must return to me. He doesn't have to return if he doesn't want to. And when he does, it reinforces the commitment and loyalty of marriage. I am worth being returned to.

Looking through these medical records, I don't see myself as a person who really had much value to anyone. As I thumb through dozens of manila file folders, dated all the way back to 2000, so much anger against the medical establishment builds in me, more than I anticipated. Five binders and a box that mark the documentation of my medical mayhem. It's like my anatomy has been shoved into a file cabinet or something.

I don't understand most of the language the so-called medical professionals used to describe me in these hundreds of pages. I see lots of jargon and abbreviations and numbers—esoteric codes that, for anyone who cared to notice, spell out in plain sight "there's nothing here."

The least someone had to do to flag my case was to look at my name and date of birth. My name, depending on the year or the specialist, was spelled differently. Sometimes my first name was hyphenated, other times my last name was spelled incorrectly with an "e" at the end. "Blancharde"—my mother's attempt to separate herself from my father, even further than she could geographically? Or was it that she was running from other things, like prior legal offenses? Anyone who cared to notice could've seen these inconsistencies, but nobody cared enough.

In addition to telling me things I already knew about certain diagnoses—the sleep apnea, allergies, asthma, epilepsy, muscular dystrophy, leukemia—the medical records provided me with a map and a timeline, not only of when my mother's Munchausen began to consume her but of how she trapped herself within it, like a spider stuck in its own web.

Seeing the dates of the medical records reminded me of how much we moved around. I see the names of certain doctors and the tests and procedures I underwent, and I'm instantly transported back to the various towns and cities we lived in between 1999 and 2015. But I was supposedly sick before that, as an infant.

Mama insisted that I stopped breathing in my sleep. She told me stories about how she was so nervous I would die, especially at nighttime, that she would lay me atop her chest while I slept so she could watch my little body rise and fall. Of course my rotten father was nowhere to be found, she'd remind me. She was the one who loved me enough to forego her own sleep, an exhausted new mother keeping watch over her baby bird.

I didn't find out until recently that once my mother told my father of my sleep apnea diagnosis, he decided to "give it another try with Dee Dee." It's just a theory, but could my supposed sleep apnea had been an attention grab to get my dad back? If so, it worked. Dad did find us a rental house, and he moved back in with Mama. Living in a loveless marriage, and working a job that kept him away for three weeks out of the month, Dad finally decided to break up for good. They divorced in 1992, just a year after my birth.

Once my parents were officially over, Dad and Kristy got engaged and then married, and my sleep apnea escalated to the point that I required an infant CPAP machine. The estrangement between my dad and me began around this time, when the narrative my mother preferred was that my father was an abusive asshole who tried to throw me across the room in a drunken stupor and then left to have a new family that he could physically and emotionally abuse. What kind of man leaves his wife and sickly infant? Mama swore that if I had been a boy, Dad wouldn't have left. For a long time, I felt bad for being the reason my father left Mama. There was nothing I could do to make myself a boy or to make myself unsick. Thank God I had my Mama there to save me.

I didn't see medical records of me visiting a doctor for sleep apnea in infanthood, or a prescription or records of where Mama got that CPAP machine. For all I know, she bought it at a garage sale or paid out of pocket for it at a medical supply store. Or worse, stole it from the hospital where she had once worked.

My medical records double as my mother's resume—being my caregiver was her primary profession, one that she figured out how to monetize.

I'm in awe of the lengths my mother went to in her efforts to convince doctors to test me for invisible symptoms. The documents I now have are reminders of prodding and poking, but it's the fear that I feel all over again, the fear of a confused little girl in the face of a constant barrage of unknown things that would happen to me.

I was so scared all the time. It creeped me out to undergo numerous sleep studies, which required me to be watched. I wanted to sleep with my mother, like we always did, instead of hooked up to machines like a rat in a lab. I was scared when they told me they would cut my abdomen so my mother could nourish me with a feeding tube. The loud darkness of the MRI machines, the gross dyes I had to have injected by needle, the looming threat of a cancer relapse. The records don't account for the unnecessary anxiety I endured for no good reason at all. I don't see "scared little girl" written anywhere in the anecdotal notes at the bottom of the pages.

Instead, I find one note: "Our favorite mother-daughter patient." I'm enraged. It's like the doctor couldn't even let me have my own patient identity. He just wrapped us into one warped person. *What does having a favorite have to do with my fake kidney disease you are testing for?* I see notations about the blood traces in my urine, and the dye I drank to test my kidneys for dysfunction. I recall vividly that day in the bathroom of the doctor's office, when Mama pricked her finger with a safety pin and let the drop of blood spill into the white paper cup I had just peed in.

The tests, of course, all came back negative. Even with the good news of healthy kidneys, my mother found a way to gain the worry and follow-up of the doctors: I had a severe allergic reaction to the kidney dye. The records indicate my mother reported this to them, and they had not actually witnessed an adverse reaction. What she falsified became fact with just a pen stroke. These medical records reveal an arsenal of weapons my mother was capable of wielding.

Had I witnessed a ruthlessness in my mother when I was smaller, when I saw her putting Roundup weed killer in her stepmother Laura's food? Was that why we suddenly left town and went to

New Orleans to live in the Ronald McDonald House, where we spent several weeks rent free? And then to Slidell, Louisiana, and then back to our Section 8 housing project in Thibodaux? Bouncing around was a way to ensure people would lose track of us, lose track of the lies, and to distance us from any chance of running into a competent human being who would call her out on her deceit.

These medical records are like a montage of my mother's disease. I see, as I review them, that she focused on asserting symptoms nobody could perceive so she couldn't be contradicted. Warning signs that were not obvious. "Gypsy-Rose has multiple medical concerns as outlined by her mother," one record states. She had to find things wrong with me that would require at least an initial examination, creating a condition for doctors to figure that they needed to take her word for it.

The devastation of Hurricane Katrina helped the doctors to do exactly that. Katrina helped my mother prey on the empathy of others, an opportunity for monetizing my medical history. With all my medical records supposedly lost in Katrina, we moved to Missouri in 2005, refugees and victims of a storm that wiped out an entire city. I was confused but not yet suspicious when Mama's storytelling escalated into a false backstory. We suddenly had dead relatives, we'd lost our home and all our possessions in Katrina, and Mama had once been a nurse. Welcomed and cared for by the sweet community of Springfield, we became local celebrities, recipients of the compassion of its people, where we were gifted a

Habitat for Humanity house on Volunteer Way. Where we lived for ten years until the night of the murder.

I notice the pattern now, in these records, the ripple effects of each of my diseases and disorders. The sleep apnea, the seizures that led to my "mental retardation," all invisible and unwitnessed, requiring no interrogation. The only true medical issue I had was a lazy eye, which was operated on. It looks like one way she unraveled the medical issues was to pick something like a seizure, and then look into the plethora of effects that could happen to the body in the aftermath and continue from there.

Another way she justified my illnesses was by claiming I had a disease-inducing chromosomal defect. Interestingly, I found a chromosome test in one of the boxes of my medical files. It was ordered in 2012 when I was already twenty years old, after a doctor could not find anything wrong with me that would explain the cornucopia of illnesses my mother claimed I had. His last-ditch effort was to consider if my ailments were due to a rare chromosomal defect. To my surprise, the results on this test indicate that I actually *do* have what's known as a microdeletion, 1q21.1, which is a chromosomal change in which a small piece of chromosome 1 is deleted in each cell.

This was news to me! Flustered, I turned to the internet to sleuth around about what this actually means. What I discovered is staggering. This microdeletion is known to "increase the risk of delayed development, intellectual disability, physical abnormalities, and neurological and psychiatric problems." Wow. What a coincidence. Every illness my mother claimed I had had fallen beneath all of these umbrellas. Except I didn't actually have a single one of them.

Was this diagnosis the smoking gun my mother used to scam the medical world? Just when I thought I had figured out the mystery, I realized how that theory just can't be true. Because I had already lived with these supposed illnesses for two decades by the time of these test results.

Exploring my medical records was supposed to demystify me, not baffle me even more. Now I had more questions than I'd had before. Does there somewhere exist a similar chromosome test, one given to me when I was born? Was this the one medical issue I had that was true? Did my mother then turn that one truth into a thousand lies? The rest of my files indicate "no abnormalities," so regardless of the actual microdeletion, I had grown up unscathed by it.

They say the best liars use a hint of truth. Either my mother knew I had this condition before the 2012 test, researched the potential outcomes, and ran with them . . . or, this one time, the disorder she claimed for me turned out to be real (though without real symptoms).

This was a rabbit hole my brain went down and I still can't climb out of. Different scenarios keep me up at night. Did she simply read too many baby books when she was pregnant with me and feared all the potential negative outcomes? Did she know she had the same genetic abnormality and presumptuously tell people she had passed it on to me?

My grandmother, Emma, holding my mom as an infant.

My mom with her birthday cake.

My mom at age 18, and her trophy,
after winning the ROTC beauty pageant.

My dad fixing his hair on his and my mom's wedding day.

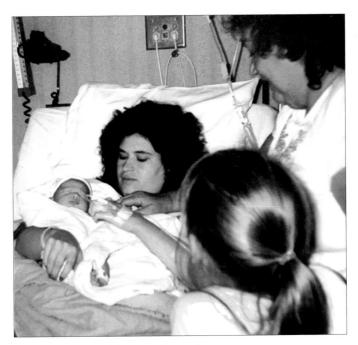

Mom and newborn me.

Mommzie Emma and me.

My dad's scratch sheet for his child support payments in 1995-96.

My dad and me at the GUMBO games during one of the
few times we saw each other when I was a child.

The "Blue House" where my mom and I lived
before my uncle inherited it.

Me, at around one year old, when life was simple.

85 Narrative:
On 10/26/09, I was dispatched to 2103 W. Volunteer Way (a location in Greene County MO) to meet with DFS and speak with an individual in regards to a child at that location.

I arrived on scene and made contact with DFS case workers Jessica Clayton and Marlena Sorenson. Sorenson informed me that there is a child, identified as Gypsy-Rose Blanchard, residing at the address with her mother, Claudine Blanchard. DFS advised that Claudine claims her daughter is paralyzed from the waist down, has MS, cancer and other medical issues. According to the DFS hotline call, St. John's Hospital contacted DFS and informed them that a doctor has checked on Gypsy and her alleged medical issues that Claudine claims Gypsy has. According to DFS, and the hotline call, a doctor could not find any symptoms that would support what Claudine alleges to be wrong with her daughter.

According to the hotline, Claudine provided different personal information on Gypsy. Due to the inconsistent birth dates and lack of medical diagnoses, DFS wanted Gypsy checked on to ensure she was not an endangered runaway or missing juvenile. They also wanted to ensure that Claudine was the biological mother to Gypsy.

DFS and I made contact with Claudine and Gypsy and spoke to them about the situation. Claudine stated they are from Louisiana and left there during hurricane Katrina and came to the Springfield, Missouri area. When confronted about all the inconsistent information that she had provided to the hospital, Claudine stated she didn't know why the birth dates and personal information were wrong.

After further investigation, it was found that Claudine had a bad marriage and got a divorce. Due to her fear of her ex-husband, Claudine had changed her daughter's information at the hospital, so that her ex-husband would not be able to find them.

Notes from the time the Department of Family Services
visited us in Springfield.

State of Missouri
Department of Corrections

Certificate of Achievement

This certificate is being presented to

Blancharde, Gypsy #1302048

For successful completion of

Impact of Crime on Victims (ICVC)
Facilitator Training

August 15-16, 2019

_____   _____
Facilitators/Supervisors

Throughout my time at Chillicothe, I signed up for multiple
twelve-week-long classes. These certificates of completion
are valuable reminders of my search for understanding.

While speaking with Jane, she stated she has known the Blanchard's for approximately ten years. Jane first met the Blanchard's when they moved here from Louisiana. She was working with the Hospitality House at Mercy Hospital, where they met when Clauddinnea would bring her daughter, Gypsy Blanchard, for treatment. When they first met, Clauddinnea told Jane that Gypsy had surgery in Louisiana, for issues with her spine. Jane said she was told the surgery was when Gypsy was a child, and it caused paralysis, making her wheelchair bound. Clauddinnea also confided in Jane that she was involved in a bad vehicle accident in Louisiana, where she suffered leg injuries, causing her to also need a wheelchair.

Jane stated she believed Clauddinnea suffered from psychological issues. Over the past ten years, the two shared many conversations in which Clauddinnea stated she was bi-polar, and thought often that people were watching her. Jane said she believed Clauddinnea filed a complaint with the Aurora, Missouri, Police Department in 2006, claiming a male was looking into the windows of her residence. I noted that a previous phone conversation I had with the Aurora Police Department, revealed all records prior to 2008 were destroyed when their data server crashed.

Clauddinnea also told Jane, during several conversations, that Clauddinnea felt their house was haunted. At one point, Clauddinnea also taped over the camera on her laptop, telling Jane she believed someone

Soon after my release from prison, I pored through my medical files. Along with them were my case files, where I discovered this police interview with Jane, a friend of my mother's, who recounts my mom's mental illness.

One of our class assignments in prison was to illustrate what our crime looked like and the impact it had on the victims. This is a picture of my Habitat for Humanity house, in a frame; the frame is cracked. In the shards of glass are all the people who were affected by my crime. And it was me using a hammer to break the picture they had in their minds. On the hammer I have Nick's name, seeing him as a tool for doing this. Not hiding behind excuses, I take accountability. This is what I did—*why* I did it didn't matter.

The prison photographer, who was also an inmate, took this photo of Ken and me right after we got engaged.

While I didn't have my father's presence in my life until now, my daughter will be blessed to have such a loving grandfather in her life. Here I am with my dad, Rod, at the gender reveal party, where Dad discovered he will have a granddaughter to teach how to fish. Photo credit: Michele Matrisciani

Nonetheless, she had used this chromosomal microdeletion, as benign as it was, to convince everyone that I had the "mind of a seven-year-old." Even though back in Golden Meadow, she said my low IQ was because of the epileptic seizures that I never had.

She said that my salivary glands were contributing to my swallowing problems, but then she also said that my swallowing had been affected by the seizures. Later, with an ENT specialist, she posited that the issues with my glands and my high-pitched voice could be related. An exploratory surgery to cut my larynx was scheduled.

The most dramatic inconsistency had to do with the use of my wheelchair.

Despite the fact that Mama told some people I needed a wheelchair because of a car accident, and others that my immobility was due to muscular dystrophy, I found a medical record from a cardiologist that stated, "She is a quadriplegic from birth and is in a wheelchair." On the same document, my date of birth is recorded as being July 1994, three years later than my real birth date.

I looked up the definition of "quadriplegic," and I was stunned that not only did Mama pass me off as not being able to walk, but she was audacious enough to claim I was paralyzed from the neck down. And still, nobody questioned her.

Making up a backstory was part of her process. She told stories, creating devastation where there was none: Both my grandfathers had died of "arterial disease." I had cancer. My father had been abusive to us. Her lies estranged me from my father, brother, and sister, and from the entire Pitre family. She even went as far as taking a baby picture of my brother Dylan, Dad and Kristy's first born, and showing it to people as her dead baby boy, who she had with my father before I was born.

She used drugs to manipulate my body to mimic certain symptoms. Before the sleep studies, she would mix Xanax with Benadryl. Could that combination have affected my breathing? She drugged me with narcotics to make me go limp and cause me brain fog. She put Orajel on my gums to make me drool, so she'd have doctors believe my salivary glands were not working properly. Before doctors' appointments, she made me really sleepy with extra doses of Keppra, which treats seizures.

My ability to take ownership of these medical records is empowering. But I am also hunting. I can't change the past or what was done to me, but I do want to know concrete answers on why they took out my teeth. I never had any reason given to me from a doctor, nor from Mama. Being reminded of all the medications and the different procedures, like going under anesthesia, isn't giving me a clear, full explanation as to why they extracted all my teeth. All I've dug up is "Mom reported tooth pain." Always, her word was gospel.

I see the records from the food allergist, noting how my mother was thorough and caring enough to bring in the food labels of ingredients and foods I supposedly had allergic reactions to: a donut, an oatmeal cookie, a chocolate chip cookie, a Dove bar. My mother is on record saying that when I was fed rice products, oats, apples, or corn, I'd have a reaction. "She has avoided milk, soy, and egg in the past," the records say.

And of course, she insisted I was allergic to sugar, even though she said I could eat some fruits, which have sugar naturally in them. It's such a dumb claim. Still, it took years for a red flag to be waved and DFS called, to no avail.

I watched a little bit of the documentary on Lifetime that we filmed while I was waiting to be released, and it was the first time I heard, from a couple of doctors, anything like, "Gypsy, if you're listening, I'm so sorry. I wish I would've acted. I feel like I failed you."

But you know, I toyed with the idea of filing a malpractice lawsuit. I have all of this evidence of negligence. Really, though, I just want to focus on my future restorative surgeries. So if I sue anyone, it will be so they pay for things they did in the past that continue to cause me to suffer in the present. My teeth are what I want back. Absent some kind of compensation, I'd have to pay out of pocket to undo things that were done to me. I'm very much still paying for their mistakes.

I'm not asking for millions of dollars. I'm just saying: Help me have enough money to pay for restorative surgery so I could at least have a little normalcy back in my life. And last I checked, they can't give me my salivary glands back.

I keep looking for where the doctors crossed the point of no return, where my records take a wrong turn into the realm of becoming life-threatening to me. It was when they started moving beyond the testing and actually acted; when they started cutting and manipulated my body, altering it and changing its healthy form forever.

The feeding tube. Supposedly, I had a fear of eating, and that claim was enough to surgically insert a silicon tube into a five-year-old. I don't recall being spoken to about this fear. Other explanations my mother gave to people regarding the tube included my cancer, an inability to swallow, and food allergies. She needed to control my nourishment to keep me safe. With every injection of Pedialyte, she chose the dosage and the feeding times, and therefore she could control my weight. After all, a sick child isn't supposed to have meat on her bones. That feeding tube kept me connected to my mother the way an umbilical cord does. She could turn the food supply on or off my whenever she wanted, like a human spigot.

I spent my entire life without any bodily autonomy. But as much as the records I now rightfully have back in my possession make me sad and angry, I also feel empowerment, and hope, and peace. As I piece together my medical mystery, uncovering truths and details that my mother withheld from me, I'm going to stay steady on the path to the future I'm on now, one lined with understanding and knowledge and self-awareness. Will that lead to forgiveness? I will have to wait and see.

I've been blessed to have been given a second chance at life. Not everyone has the opportunity to bring awareness to a horrible situation—or create meaning where there once was none. This is the good thing about being public: having the ability to reach a lot of people with a message of positivity.

I don't want to be the victim *and* the perpetrator any longer. I want to have influence; maybe even go to the Capitol and get some laws in place, get some things changed. For starters, I'd create oversight, so doctors can be kept accountable for doing harm and for being inept. Maybe this is my purpose. By exercising my purpose, I can ensure doctors are more observant of their patients' care and get trained to look for red flags. My medical history was not a red flag, though. It was a goddamn red banner that read HOW COULD YOU NOT KNOW? How many people saw my real birth date on my Medicaid card and just disregarded it, thinking: *Oh, look, a typo. Oh well.*

My mother once had to make a preemptive strike to a receptionist at the doctor's office, who must have looked at the card askance. "Oh, yes," she said, with a smile. "Her card says she was born in ninety-one, but it's actually nineteen ninety-five."

And that, y'all, was good enough for them.

By the time we got to the ENT to "explore" the problem of my squeaky voice, the doctors had been conditioned to not question such a knowledgeable, doting mother. Or maybe they didn't want to face her attitude, the way family members did when they questioned her about my health. So a surgery was recommended to open up my throat to take a peek at my larynx. No biggie.

After the beating in the alley; the two weeks tied to the bed; the BB gun; the night in the shed; a lifetime of lies, spells, isolation, starvation, emotional manipulation, and medical procedures with life-changing side effects; this unnecessary *exploratory* surgery on my voice box felt most threatening to me. Any slip of the hand could leave me voiceless, mute, forever. This is what I believed. This is what I felt. This is when the thought finally came: *It's me or her.*

Hysterical, I pleaded with her to reconsider the surgery. There was no discussion, as usual. When we got home from that appointment with the ENT, I took three oxy and craved the fantasy world Nick and I lived in. I messaged him.

"Do you remember when you told me you'd protect me from people who want to hurt me?" I asked Nick over text.

"Yes, darling."

"Will you still protect me?"

"Yes," Nick answered.

"Even from my mother?"

"Yes."

THIRTEEN

Negotiations

"You have to come get me," I begged Nick. The plan was for him to get back on a bus and take me to his home in Wisconsin to live with him and his mom and stepdad. Nick had a private room with a bathroom all his own upstairs, so we'd be comfortable enough and have privacy. Nick said his mother welcomed me but wouldn't give him the money to come back to Missouri. She didn't know too much about my situation. She talked to Nick about our relationship as if we were any other twentysomething couple in love and miles apart. Her advice to him was that couples take turns in the relationship, so it was my turn to reciprocate for the visit he took when we met at the movie theater a few months earlier. She told Nick that if I really loved him, I would make the trip to Wisconsin. "Gypsy needs to come to Wisconsin this time," Nick's mother said.

A little something clicked in my head. I guess because it was so natural for his mother to assume I would just go to him for a visit, as if life were that simple and I could go about doing things that are expected to be done by everyone in the world, except me. Hearing it this way, it just all clicked. *I'm not free to make my own choices in life. Life should be that simple, and mine's not.* I homed in on the devastating notion that I had this open invitation and opportunity to visit Nick, his mother supporting our love. And I couldn't do a damn thing.

We felt like our relationship was on the brink of collapse.

We believed we'd tried everything to be together, and now it was a matter of taking extreme measures.

We worried the shed incident would lead to something worse for me.

"We need to think of a new option," Nick said.

I agreed. And then I made the suggestion, to which Nick said, "Victor can do it. But you need to be the one to beg him."

So, I sent a message to Victor on Facebook, and the exchange went something along the lines of:

"Victor, will you please do the deed?"

"Yes, my submissive, I will do the deed for you, but it will be done my way and how I want. My one condition to do the deed, because you are too weak to do this yourself, I want to rape your mother."

"No."

"HOW THE FUCK AM I SUPPOSED TO DO THIS,
AND HOW DARE YOU ASK ME TO DO THIS AND
YOU WON'T GIVE ME THE ONE THING I ASK FOR?"

"I'll let you rape me instead."

"Then know I am going to rape you after it's done."

"Okay."

"You will go to the bathroom. I will scratch on the
door. The scratch is the code for 'it's over.'"

"Okay."

"You will be clean and shaved and naked. And
then I will rape you."

"Okay."

The contract sealed, our subsequent conversations turned strategic. How could "the deed" be done? How can he kill my mother so I can be free?

"Arson? Burn up the house?" Nick suggested. "Knock over a candle and it will look like an accident."

"No, there's too many things that can go wrong," I answered.

"Roundup or arsenic?"

"No," I said, "poison is slow and shuts the body down. Too brutal. If it's going to happen, I want it quick and painless."

"What about a gun? Victor can shoot her," Nick suggested.

I researched how I could get a gun, but information online revealed that I needed a state-issued ID, which I didn't have.

"How about a knife?" Nick wrote as a caption to a picture of a large fillet knife he sent me. It was like a fucking machete.

"No, I'm not getting you that," I said.

"My rule is you will buy it."

Nick said he wanted to strangle my mother and stab her and feed her body to pigs.

"We don't want DNA or a body," he said. "We can dump her at a pig farm. Pigs eat anything."

I asked nicely that we just make it quick and painless. But it's like he didn't hear me. "Get triple-locking handcuffs, a ball gag, and a Taser, so I can torture her a little."

I looked online for what he suggested, and I was like, "I said painless." That's when he told me to get duct tape instead. The final plan was I'd steal a large kitchen knife from Walmart. He could rape me when he was done. He would leave her body in her bed. Then we'd slip off to Wisconsin to live our quiet life. I thought we had it all settled, and then he had an idea.

Nick said he wanted to load my mother's dead body into our Ford Windstar, rape her with a condom, and then afterward, demand that I suck his semen from it, and then drop her body at a pig farm.

"That's absolutely disgusting," I said. "I don't want to do that."

He reminded me that I was well aware of Victor's demented fantasies and that I couldn't change him now. Then I reminded him that my ninety-five-pound body would never be able to move the dead weight of a two-hundred-pound woman. When we both realized that the laws of physics were against us, the unspoken plan was to leave her where she was.

He could've called the cops. I could have called the cops. He could've told his mother what was going on, but neither of us did. The only thing that ran through my head was my life was at stake. I had already tried to run away from home—twice. She found me, brought me back, and made it worse for me. She had paperwork saying I was mentally incompetent, so I thought she'd just tell the cops the same thing if I dialed 911. The police would probably just bring me back to her. DFS had already made their visit, never to return. She told me my entire family consisted of shitheads and that my father was abusive to his new kids. Brilliant minds in science and medicine had been duped, and the school system didn't seem to notice I wasn't being educated. So, in my brain, I was thinking about all the ways that I had already tried and failed. And of all the experts in their respective fields, all the authority figures—doctors, social workers, clergy, philanthropists—who had been useless in detecting any abuse or helping me in any positive way.

What was in Nick's brain? I don't know for sure, but it felt like I was being used to help him live out this fantasy as if he was playing around with characters that he created in his mind or in a video game. And some of them were evil killers, and maybe it might be fun for him to play around with that darker side of life. Were we using each other?

With hindsight, I wish Nick had been someone different. A man, perhaps, who would've stopped me in my tracks, told me it was going to be okay, and that he'd help me find my dad or call the police or at least tell his family to help me. I wish the man I met online would've been able to help me see that desperate times do not call for desperate measures; that when you love someone you help them rise above their circumstances instead of taking the lowest way out. I wish the man I met online hadn't been as irrational, as isolated, and as disturbed as I had been in that very moment. Maybe none of this would have happened if I had still been talking to Dan? Maybe my mother would still be alive if she allowed me at least one "phone a friend"? Maybe if I had been educated or without a cocktail of prescription drugs, my rational brain would've worked better?

I will never know.

FOURTEEN

June 9, 2015

It's my last Saturday morning in prison. The passing of time has stopped as suddenly as a summer rain in the South. My morning ritual, drinking instant coffee and breaking off the corner of a Pop-Tart, will soon be a memory. As of next Saturday, I'll be in a home, my home, learning how to brew real coffee in a percolator. I have so much to learn about, even the most basic things. Like, how do I like my eggs? Or do I even like eggs? Which side of the bed do I prefer? Will I pick the side I slept on with my mother? Or will I do the opposite? Which is to say, either decision will be equally governed by her. What television shows will I like? Which series will I binge-watch first? Will I go for a health physical? How will I find the right therapist? Will making love freak me out? Next Saturday I will be on the incline of a learning curve with slopes that range from mundane to serious. Will there be mere distractions from the great regret of my life? Or will the curves be more like a roller coaster of reminders?

On this last weekend spent at Chillicothe, I feel stiller than ever. Someone told me to enjoy the calm, because this might be the quietest and most private time I will have for a very long time. I know I'll be meeting the press, and I'll be asked a million questions. Some people will be happy for me; others will hate me. Both groups will swap positions until they lose interest. I get it. I've done it myself. I've been fascinated over people, wondered what made them do things, imagined how they feel about their choices. But like a toddler catching the glimpse of a new shiny toy, I've turned my attention to the next exciting thing.

As part of my life penance, I will be accountable for my crime. However, there is one part of my story that I will leave locked up behind bars at Chillicothe. I want to talk about it here, in this book, so I know I've preserved the important details, along with validating the suffering endured by my mother in her final moments.

June 9, 2015. I wanted the circumstances I was living in to go away forever. When I thought of her, it was as an obstacle. *You are the obstacle. What do I have to do to get past you?*

I let Nick into my house to remove my obstacle.

Mama slept with her baby pillow, the one she had since she was literally an infant. My mother carried that baby pillow in a larger pillowcase, like a potato dropped in a sack, as a way to preserve the timeline of her existence trapped in a yellow-stained residue of spit-up, tears, sweat, and, soon enough, blood. And then she put that into another pillowcase and into another, forming what looked like lumpy mashed potatoes.

The night my mother was going to die, I remember slowing the evening down. I think people would describe it as being "in the moment." I took in my mother in a way I never had. I smelled that pillow, imprinting her scent in my memory, like a hunting dog. I cried in the pillow as I spoke to it, saying, "I'm sorry. But this is something I have to do." I wiped my tears, got back in my wheelchair, and found her in the kitchen as she prepared my dinner. I wheeled myself up to the back of her and hugged her waist. When she turned, she could see my eyes were a little wet.

"I love you," I said.

"Baby," she answered, "I love you too. But I'm not dead yet."

Was she really reading my mind?

I told Nick I'd leave surgical gloves outside for him, and to text me when he was ready to come inside. I'd hand the knife to him then. I promised I'd paint my nails pink for him, so after dinner my mother and I ran an errand at Walmart, watched *Merlin,* and painted each other's nails in liquid cotton candy.

I kept an eye on the clock so I could text him from a secret phone when I knew she was sleeping. It was 1:30 AM when I wrote him "She's asleep." I wasn't focused on what he would need to do to remove the obstacle. I just focused on the aftermath, the freedom. Would we get a dog or a cat? There was a moment when I grimaced at the thought of her being strong enough to struggle.

"Okay, getting a cab now," Nick texted back.

I got out of our bed, because I still slept with my mother; I got into the electric wheelchair and went to pee and took three more Vicodin. I waited for the next text.

"I'm here."

I rolled my wheelchair to the door and let Nick in. I still didn't dare walk, as my mother could wake at any point.

"Okay, where's the knife?" Nick asked, all business, not noticing my nails still smelled of the pink lacquer. He was dressed in very dark sweatpants, a black graphic T-shirt with scary clowns, and a black zippered hoodie. I pulled the large kitchen knife from the couch cushion, where I had tried to hide so many objects from her. Nick ordered, "Get your ass to the bathroom."

"Yes, Sir."

I went to the bathroom, sat on the floor, and covered my ears. Except I heard. I heard everything.

Nick entered the room soundlessly because there was no bedroom door, so when she finally woke up it must have been because he was standing over her, not because of any noise. She was startled. And I remember hearing her as if her voice was muffled because I was a couple of doors down the hall with the door closed. But it sounded like she said, "Who are you?"

In Nick's arrest interview, he claimed he said something like, "I am death. You will die now." But I didn't hear that. I just heard the screaming. And then I lay in the fetal position with my hands pressed hard over my ears. But I could still hear things.

"Stop!" I heard her say. "Enough, enough, please. Enough."

There was a pause in the stabbing. And then it sounded like she may have had a pool of blood in her mouth because I heard her say with a gargle, "Gypsy. Gypsy."

I didn't answer. I didn't go to her. I just stayed very, very still. I was trying to focus on my breathing. There weren't thoughts going through my head at all. It was like I was locked inside a cloud, with the out-of-reach Earth spinning below me. Nothing was real. I was a simulation, as I focused on taking my next breath, and the next. And then I heard one sharp, "Help me!"

During the trial it came out that Nick had cut the back of her neck, so I imagine that shrill of pain came then. My father and Kristy, along with my attorney, Mike Stanfield, kept the details and the photos far away from me. So the first time I learned the level of brutality was at Nick's trial. I remember being afraid I would vomit because in my mind, her death didn't look like the crime-scene photos. My brain had created a reality that didn't exist.

After that sharp "Help me," there was total silence. There was nothing more after that.

According to a case supplement report, a fellow inmate of Nick's at Greene County Jail told investigators that Nick began talking to him about what it was like to kill my mother. The report says, "Godejohn said it made him feel good as he was stabbing her and said he would do it again if needed for Gypsy." The inmate, who was looking to help his own legal case by snitching, also said that when my mother resisted, Nick kept stabbing her, saying "something like 'death is calling to you; stop fighting.'"

The attorneys said that the laceration at the back of her neck was deep enough that she was almost decapitated. Even though I have not looked at the photos of my mother, the image of her maimed body will never leave me. He had toyed with her. I hadn't asked for that.

Nick didn't come straight for me. Instead, he went to the kitchen to wipe off the knife with a paper towel, and he removed the blue surgical gloves, the same kind of gloves Mama had used to administer treatment to me. I was stripped down and in the bathtub, where I ran some water, shaved my legs, shaved my vagina, and then wiped myself off.

Nick scratched on the door. The signal. And that was it.

Stark naked, I opened the door for him. And he was standing there with the knife in his hand. It was wrapped in a paper towel. He walked into the bathroom, set the knife on the counter by the sink, and stretched his arms out, wanting me to hug him. And so, I gave him a hug.

"Say thank you."

"Thank you, Sir," I repeated, wondering when the relief would come.

I was shivering at that point. Nick had a paper towel around his finger, which was cut and bleeding.

"Clean me up," Nick ordered.

"Yes, Sir." I grabbed the box of Band-Aids.

I wiped the blood off his finger with an alcohol swab, the same way I'd tended to my mother's wounds after I shot her with the BB gun. I dabbed the droplet of blood on his tennis shoe. I wiped away the red handprint that wrapped around Nick's forearm.

After I got him cleaned up, we sat there in the bathroom for a second, just holding each other. His steadiness felt good as I shivered.

"Go to your bedroom," Nick ordered.

With my head bowed, I slowly walked to my bedroom. I never sat in a wheelchair again. I felt exposed and vulnerable in my nakedness, my baldness, and my gummy mouth. Nick had ordered me not to wear my wig or dentures. He wanted me stripped of everything. I resembled an alien from one of his many extraterrestrial nations that he colluded with in his various fantasy worlds and realms. As I passed my mother's bedroom, I didn't look in directly. But peripherally, I saw mounds of blankets on the bed and bags of clothes. She was buried in her own chaos.

"Get all of these stuffed animals off the bed," Nick said as he followed me into my pink princess room.

"Yes, Sir."

"Get on the bed."

I lay supine on the bed as he took off his pants and straddled me, his legs pinning down mine. Then he put his arms around my neck and began to choke me. I just remember feeling pain from him holding me down. And at that point, I feel like there may have been penetration, but I don't remember that. I just remember crying. I remember trying to scream for my mom, but I didn't have enough air. *This is not what I agreed to.*

"Stop, stop," I begged Nick. But he didn't. He just continued to choke me, one hand on my throat, one hand holding down my wrists above my head.

I don't know what I was thinking when I agreed to let Nick rape me, but I know I didn't believe it was going to be a real rape. I thought, at worst, Nick would just pronounce aloud over and over that he was raping me or something. Like dirty talk or kink. But I was feeling pressure and sharp pains, like he was trying to stuff himself inside me just like he had tried to in the movie theater bathroom.

I kept saying "stop," which, looking back, I realize was only playing into his rape fantasy. After all, isn't nonconsent the definition of rape?

"I don't hear you saying thank you, my submissive," Nick kept saying. He wanted me to be indebted to him and in reverence to him for doing "the deed."

He released some pressure from his grip on my neck, enabling me to utter, "Thank you, Sir," after which he still didn't seem aroused. I didn't want any of this to be happening. I felt like he was way too rough, biting me, strangling me. I felt like he didn't care about me or anything; that he was living out his greatest fantasy. And I feared that if I did not go along with it, if I found a way to wiggle out from beneath him, he'd go into the room across the hall and rape my mother's dead body.

And I didn't want that.

At Nick's trial, the defense asked me if Nick raped me. And I said no, because I felt like that's what I had to say. I heard the attorney say to me, "You agreed to it. You said that you knew you'd be raped that night, so you wanted it."

When you hear something like that, you know no matter what you say, even if it's how much it hurt, how many times you said "stop," or "no," or cried, the interrogators are looking for one answer—one that affirms their line of questioning. So, regretfully, I said, no; he didn't rape me. But to me, it was rape. I said no. I said stop. I cried for my mom, my mom who was dead.

There wasn't a moment when Nick finished, per se. There was no moan, or release, or semen to wipe off. He just stopped. He said later he wasn't getting any pleasure. There is a lapse in my memory, so I don't know if I blacked out or just passed out from exhaustion, but the next thing I remember is Nick picking out some clothes for me and stuffing them in a suitcase. The sound of the zipper felt so final.

While we waited for the taxi to arrive, Nick ordered me to clean the little bits of blood trailing from my mom's room to the kitchen, where he initially washed himself off. I took some baby wipes and cleaned the blood spots up, not thinking about their origin. I grabbed my mother's money pouch with four thousand dollars in it and the rest of the Vicodin and oxy.

"Say thank you, Sir."

"Thank you, Sir."

I removed pictures from the walls and put them all in trash bags, which we took out to the curb. My logic was that if there were no pictures of me, maybe nobody would know I lived there, and everyone would forget all about me. I imagined that when the police found her, they'd write in their notepads that Clauddine "Dee Dee" Blanchard was just a single woman living in the world, alone, all by herself.

In many ways, she had been.

FIFTEEN

The Hideout from Hell

Nick had booked a room at Days Inn in Springfield. It was dawn by the time we checked in. The plan was to take the bus to Wisconsin later that day, except there weren't two bus tickets available until days later, on June 12. So we holed up in the hotel, ordering pizza every day, while I ate painkillers in between meals. I was high as a kite and didn't think about what would happen when I ran out of the oxy.

It recently crossed my mind that Nick and me getting caught may have prevented me from going to dangerous lengths in order to keep getting my fix. Would I have wound up with a laced street-grade pill or upped my game with a more intense drug of choice? My drug use could've led to my own death.

During the trial, a damning video of Nick that I recorded on my phone was shown. I giggled incessantly while saying, "He's eating a brownie. Later, he'll be eating me."

Watching the entire courtroom see that video at Nick's trial was more humiliating than I can describe. But I listen to that recording now, and it's so obvious I'm in la-la land. In fact, I was high all the way through my initial interrogation in Wisconsin.

The morning we were to finally depart from the bus depot, Nick and I decided to discard the murder weapon. At first, he suggested that I put it in my backpack and take it on the bus ride back to Wisconsin. I had never been on a bus and was afraid I'd have to pass through metal detectors, so I said, "Let's mail it." I didn't think it would be different than when people purchase kitchen knives on the internet and have them shipped. No big deal. So, we put the knife in a manila envelope and mailed it to Nick's parents' house. I even put my return address on it. Reality was not a place I resided in. The knife made it safe and sound to its destination and was eventually recovered by detectives. It was used as evidence against us both after it was found hidden in Nick's closet.

After we dropped off our mail, we ate at the Waffle House. I wasn't used to eating or drinking, and the drugs made me nauseous, so the short stack and chocolate milk I ordered made me sick to my stomach. One of the legitimate medical conditions I have is lactose intolerance, so I was doubled over in pain. We had to go back to the room so I could lie down before our long trip to Big Bend.

In my delusional mind, I was preparing to meet the love of my life's family. I wanted to make a good impression on his mother. I felt bad that we had to lie to her, telling her that the reason I was coming to live with them, and why it was so urgent that Nick come to get me, was because my mother had kicked me out of the house. Nick's mother thought she was providing me refuge from a homeless shelter. I hadn't even met her yet, and I had already betrayed her kindness.

The entire time with Nick's family, over the course of about two days, we stayed upstairs in Nick's room. His mom, stepdad, and eight-year-old brother didn't bother us much. Nick didn't drive, so we walked to the gas station for drinks and snacks. But other than that, he wanted me naked in his room the entire time. Being naked and in bed were his orders, and as his submissive, I obliged. He didn't want to have sex with me or anything; he just demanded that when I was in his presence, I be naked.

After the first night, I looked around his room and was disgusted by dirty clothes, wrappers, and moldy food. He hoarded like my mom had, except she didn't have old food lying around. I tried to ignore the crusty sheets and the sweat-stained comforter. When I asked him to use his shower, I remember thinking I hadn't seen him shower since the moment he arrived at my mother's house. Not once in the hotel and not once we got to his home.

Observing more of his lifestyle, I began to question how long I could live there. It was the first time I had any foresight. *How would we live? Would I get a job? What would I do day after day?*

MY TIME TO STAND

Without an anchor or a compass, I wanted my mother. And then I washed that thought right away with a Xanax and half an oxy, rationing them now.

While Nick and I quarantined in his room, my mind wandered. We didn't have a plan for the aftermath. *What if nobody found her body? What if the police never wrote anything in the notepad and she just decomposed, or worse, our hungry cats feasted on her?* Frantic, it became urgent for me to figure out a way to get someone to go over to the house, to find her, and to bury her, like she said she had wanted once she passed. "Don't you dare cremate me," she'd say. "You stick me in the ground. I get enough hot flashes as it is."

I logged on to mine and Dee Dee's joint Facebook account and changed the status to: That Bitch is Dead.

It was the complete opposite logic of removing the pictures of myself from the wall. Now, instead of wiping clean my existence, I hoped to lure people in because they knew of my existence and that I'd never post such a thing.

Almost immediately, people thought we were hacked and messaged us asking if everything was okay. One person even wondered if we were watching a movie. Worried that nobody was concerned enough, I elaborated, posting: I fucken SLASHED THAT FAT PIG AND RAPED HER SWEET INNOCENT DAUGHTER. HER SCREAM WAS SOOOO FUCKEN LOUD. LOL.

The police were called, and the search for me began. Unbeknownst to me, the media went wild with the story.

Our neighbor Aleah knew about my secret boyfriend and Facebook page, after I had a rare moment with her alone and confided in her, trying to connect with a girl my age on subject matter I guessed was relatable: boys. She was so worried—another one of my betrayals that still haunts me. Aleah was kind and generous and told detectives about my online boyfriend. It didn't take long for the police to trace my laptop's IP address to Nick's home.

On June 15, 2015, five days after the murder, armored police vehicles and what looked like a SWAT team surrounded Nick's family's house, treating the situation as a kidnapping. I can't imagine the fear and confusion that came over Nick's family, especially his little brother, as the police removed them from their own home. Then over a loudspeaker, we heard, "Nick Godejohn, come out with your hands above your head."

I looked at Nick. He looked at me. We were both naked. Robotically, quietly, we got dressed. Hearing a forceful voice call out Nick's name, like he was a known fugitive, was surreal, dreamlike. I didn't think yet that I was in trouble, but I also didn't know what our next move would be.

"Come here," Nick said, pointing to where he was standing in front of his closet. We both got into the closet, locked the door, and sat.

"What are we going to do?" I asked Nick, my only guiding light.

"We just stick to the story. Your mom kicked you out, you were on the streets, and I came to get you to live with us. We stick to that story, no matter what."

Realizing we were about to be separated, I began to tremble. The gravity of losing him pulled on my heart.

"Okay," I answered. "Stick to the story. But I promise, I'm going to get you the best lawyer money can buy with the four grand."

We sealed our pact with a kiss.

Nick let me go down the stairs to the front door first. I remember being at the landing before taking my first step and seeing all of the police in military gear, like you would see on the news about troops in Afghanistan. I was about to descend into a sea of bulletproof vests and helmets and guns. The guns had lasers on them. The lasers were pointed at me.

"Hold your fire! Don't shoot. Don't shoot," several voices collided. They hadn't expected me to come down first. "Keep your hands where we can see them."

Instinctively, I put my arms up like a goalpost. "I'm okay, I'm okay," I kept saying. "I'm unarmed. I'm coming down."

The instant I appeared at the front door, a hand yanked me, like a cane yanks a bad act off a stage. I was swooped away by my shoulders, carried off, as if my kidnapper was at my heels.

They cuffed me behind my back and sat me down on the hood of a police car, firing off question after question. "What's your name?" "How old are you?" "What's your social security number?"

I told them I was Gypsy-Rose Blanchard, with an *e* at the end, and that I was nineteen. (I was really about a month shy of twenty-four, the same age my mother was when she had me.) I had no clue about my social security number.

The questions continued, "Does he have any weapons? Any bombs? Has he hurt you?"

I told them he didn't, waiting for Nick's silhouette to appear in the doorframe. Then I saw several police officers holding on to him and body slamming him onto the concrete where they cuffed him. And I remember him hollering, "Hey, you're hurting me."

We were taken in separate police cars to the precinct, where Nick and I would wait for Missouri detectives to fly to Wisconsin to take over the case. The room I waited in had a comfortable couch, and I remember a pillow in the shape of a fish. There was a guard outside who I babbled to. I just kept talking and talking out of nervousness, telling him all about my trips to Disney World. For four hours I went on and on about every movie in the *Harry Potter* series. At this point, there were nice people asking me about the different medications I was taking. They were concerned I hadn't taken my dosage of Keppra, my seizure medication, so they managed to get me some, which always made me sleepy. I napped while I waited.

It took ten minutes for Nick to give me up. I didn't trail too far behind that. Detective Stan Hancock questioned me, while Nick had a female detective, Angela Maholy, question him. We stuck to the story as long as a wet noodle sticks to a wall, and then it was every man for himself.

Looking at the footage of me in the interview room, I don't recognize or recall myself. It's almost like being out of body, seeing yourself the way everyone else sees you—the way you really are.

I don't like the girl I see. But I understand now, we are naturally wired for self-preservation. As full of holes as my responses were, I was trying to build my own life raft.

The detectives bet on a bluff, telling Nick that I had ratted him out. Then they sat back and let the he said–she said game begin. Nick named me the mastermind. I named him the monster. He said he was trying to save me from abuse. I said my mother was my best friend. He said I bought the knife, gave him the gloves, rounded up duct tape. I said he had a dark side and wanted to feed her to pigs and rape her dead body. He said my mother made people think I was sick. I said Nick was sick.

The seasoned detectives knew soon enough we'd implode, as we moved facts around like chess pieces on a board controlled by expert opponents.

As Hancock moved from questioning to probing, I could feel the temperature of the water rising, boiling me alive. *I'm in trouble.* Finally, I realized it, and as such, I panicked. My sentences made no sense. Most of the time, I didn't even finish them. "But she hated him," "She despised . . . ," "She wouldn't . . . ," "It's just that . . ."

I wasn't sure how to articulate that I just wanted to be free. That it was her or me, do or die. She was going to hurt me. She was going to slit my throat. She was going to take my voice. *Would they listen to me? Would they understand it? Would they care? Why would they?* I didn't trust a soul, and once Hancock told me Nick blamed it all on me, I mourned the loss of the trust I had for him.

As I became undone, Hancock spoke in metaphors. Something like, "This is your chance to write your own story. You're the pen. And I won't know anything until you tell me what happened. Why did you do this?"

"I didn't," I cried. "I didn't."

I was lying. But I was telling the truth.

SIXTEEN

County Jail

By the time I asked for a lawyer, Nick and I had already been charged with the exact same crime: first-degree murder, with armed criminal action, and we were moved to Waukesha County Jail. It didn't matter whose hand held the knife or whose impulse it was to try to cut a dead woman's head off. The police didn't see a distinction between Nick and me. Outside of Nick's house, sitting on the police car, I was never read my Miranda rights, so I hadn't thought I was under arrest. If I had watched detective shows instead of the Disney Channel, maybe I would've known to lawyer up. But I'm glad I didn't. I needed what happened next to happen.

It turned out that my little nest egg of four thousand dollars wasn't enough to retain an OJ dream team, so I was assigned a public defender who would see me through an arraignment, until

I would be extradited to Missouri, where I would begin to defend my case. During those three days in County, I didn't know who to call for help, other than Nick. *Who else do I have in this world, other than him?* I didn't have any phone numbers. The only number I knew was my own, and nobody was there.

I was completely unaware of the sensation our arrest was making on national news, which is how my aunt Celeste—and pretty much every estranged family member—found out. Celeste is my dad's younger sister, who I vaguely remembered, but I jumped at the chance to call her after she contacted my public defender with her phone number. So my "one phone call" was to Aunt Celeste.

Picking up the receiver to dial her number, my stomach was a battleground where hope and dread duked it out. I dreaded the awkwardness of being vulnerable to a stranger, but I held tightly to hope that she would be able to guide me, to help me.

"I know you don't really know me," I said, leaning against the sticky beige wall of the jail, "but I'm in a lot of trouble."

"Gypsy, do you know your dad's number?" Celeste's voice was shaky, but kind. I wished I could've trusted her completely, but I wasn't sure if she had an ulterior motive for reaching out. My mother had told me so many shitty things about every single one of my family members, I found it impossible to consider that Celeste could be genuinely concerned for a niece who was a perfect stranger. I tried to be gracious when she gave me my dad's phone number, but I kept her at arm's length.

"The next phone call you get to make," Celeste said, "call your dad."

As I waited for permission to make another call, I imagined all the ways the conversation between my dad and me could go. I had no connection to him. We didn't know each other. He was an acquaintance at best. Parents and children don't need words to know what's going on inside. Their shared experience is a language that transcends words. That wasn't the case for me and my dad. He didn't know me well enough to know my proclivities, to gauge my mental or emotional state. Again, dread and hope returned in their circular duel, as I picked up the phone and dialed my father. *Would he be home? Was he waiting for my call? Did he even know that Celeste told me to call him? What if he's angry at me? What if he hates me? After all this time, why would he help me now?*

"Hello?" he said, as it were a question.

I didn't let him get a word in. My rambling took up all the space on the phone line, so I could postpone hearing his response, his rejection.

"Daddy," I said, "I'm innocent. I didn't do it. Don't believe what's on the TV because I would never hurt Mama and I'm really scared and I know we haven't had a chance to really talk alone all these years but I don't know what to do, Daddy."

Up to this point, my dad and I had never had a private phone call, nor a phone conversation that went beyond the superficial small talk that acquaintances do about the weather or football. This was the first time I spoke to him without my mother hovering and feeding me lines, telling me what to say and how to say it. And this was no small talk.

Dad was so unbelievably calm. His voice was steady. I found myself wishing I could surrender to his lead. Not the way a submissive does, but the way a little girl feels safe doing so around her daddy.

"It's okay, don't worry, okay?" Dad said, in his buttery Cajun accent. "Just hang tight. We, we'll get you through this."

I so desperately wished I could trust him. *What's wrong with me?*

My dad's job as a trawler requires him to remain calm when the sea tries to swallow a crew whole. Even though he was grappling with his own shock, confusion, and anger about the scam that defined his life, my dad planted his feet behind the captain's wheel, navigating me. The way he never was allowed to when Mama was around.

We said our goodbyes. Soon I'd see him in Missouri, when we could begin working with my Missouri-appointed public defender, Mike Stanfield.

While I waited to be transported to Missouri, I was still in the phase where I believed Nick loved me and I loved him. We would accidentally pass each other in county jail, with our attorneys shielding us from making eye contact. I was angry and sad because I felt betrayed by his interrogation video. I really thought he would never sell me out. But even though I was hurt, I still couldn't help worrying about what was going to happen to him.

We wrote to each other through a metal grate in the wall in the recreation room. In the mornings, the women used the rec room; and in the afternoon, the men occupied it. We would leave letters for each other to find behind the grate.

"I need you to be brave," Nick wrote.

"I'm sorry you are going through this," I wrote back.

In one letter, he quoted Ephesians 5, which he translated as something like, "Wives are supposed to be submissive to their husbands."

With all that was going on, he still wanted to play games.

Love is patient and kind, not dominant or submissive. I don't recall the Bible saying love is deviant and humiliating, but before the crime, I mistook these behaviors for attention, and any attention at all made me feel seen and beautiful. Being submissive was also familiar. My mother had wanted an infant; Nick wanted a slave. Both required them dominating me and me letting them.

I tried to hang on to what I thought was a bond of forever love and deep intimacy. We'd leave etchings on the wall: "NPG luvs GB." My first letter was an apology for getting him into this mess. I was still thinking he loved me enough to save me from what had been going on, and I wanted him to know that I knew what he sacrificed for me.

The van that transported me from Wisconsin back to Missouri had seats made of plastic, shaped in the opposite form of your butt. It was like sitting on a clamshell for two days. My hands were hand-cuffed behind my back and my feet shackled, as I fidgeted my tail-bone around, failing to find a place to fit in the curve of the seat. Two men who were being dropped in St. Paul, Minnesota, also cuffed and shackled, sat directly across from me. As if we were in an elevator together, I tried to look anywhere around the van but at them.

"Girl," one of the men said, "you all over the news. You going to death row."

This was my first glimpse of the public attention my case would attract. Even prisoners without access to television knew about Nick and me. They were having a good time fucking with me, going on and on about my fate, watching me freak out.

After the van dropped them in St. Paul, we stopped at McDon-ald's, where I ate biscuits and gravy for the first time. I only remem-bered eating biscuits with Daddy Claude, but we always had butter. So even on this cold, rainy, damp drive of doom, I experienced something deliciously new. For Southerners, biscuits and gravy rep-resent the simple life—sweet and salty. I'm glad I savored the taste, because that was as good as it was going to get for a very long time.

SEVENTEEN

Comme On Fait Son Lit, On Se Couche

You've made your bed, now lie on it.

People were reeling. I could walk. I could eat. The wheelchair was an unnecessary prop. The feeding tube, a mirage. While it would've been safe to assume all of my other ailments were fake, it would've been dangerous not to treat me for them, at least until they could confirm what was real and what wasn't. In order to do that, once I got to Greene County Jail, I was placed under surveillance. Of course, I didn't know this at the time. Nothing was explained. I was cuffed and shackled and at the mercy of the people who towed me around.

What meds did I really need? What diseases did I really have? What symptoms or withdrawals was I exhibiting? Without access to a designated "medical watch," where doctors could run tests or observe me or analyze my medical records, authorities were left to put me on suicide watch. It took me about seven seconds to learn that sending a dejected person to such a place only puts them closer to the brink, not the other way around.

County jail is a despicable place. It was dirty and crowded, the food was expired and toxic, and the people were ruthless, no matter the tier they were on. Tier 1 was for holding prisoners charged with lesser crimes, like drug offenses and prostitution. The women there shared an open bay pod, a dormitory-style area with several bunk beds, a communal area, and shared facilities.

People charged with more heinous and violent crimes, like murder, were housed on Tier 2. That's where they put me. All the inmates at County have not yet had their day in court. Idle, they await their fate. Boredom plus lockup is not a good combination. I'd wait more than a year to see a judge and receive my sentence. Until then, I learned quickly how to protect myself from the horrors of living among hopeless and desperate criminals, many of whom were repeat offenders; many had not much to lose.

Maybe whoever was calling the shots thought I'd be safer in a segregated suicide watch, because I'd be separated from the rest of the population who had heard about my case and might harass me. Or maybe it was to protect me from violence. I had gone from living a sheltered, isolated life to living with wolves that showed their teeth to assert their power, to fill their boredom, and to stay alive themselves. I was sent to the segregated cellblock without explanation. I thought they were trying to torture me, teach me a lesson. I kept thinking about the two men in the van to St. Paul. *Maybe this is a prequel to death row.*

Barefoot, I was forced to wear a dark-green smock with nothing underneath. If I got my period, they'd give out special underwear, not much different from the Pull-Ups my mother put me in. They delivered me to a concrete-and-brick cell about six feet by six feet, with one toilet and two naked ladies. At the time, I didn't know why they weren't wearing smocks. Soon enough I'd figure out the smocks could be used as nooses.

Suicide watch doubled as a psych ward. Did they think I was mentally unstable? I wasn't showing signs of a breakdown, but maybe, to them, that was a telltale sign of psychosis? Maybe I wasn't reacting because I had lost contact with reality? Was I taking it all too well, adjusting better than they thought I should? Upon my arrest and transport, I'd exhibited no freaking out or attempts to hurt myself or others. Was I somehow carrying my dad's steadfastness with me? Or maybe it was just shock. Or denial. Probably all of it. Possibly none of it. Regardless, they must have thought I was crazy because my roommates certainly were not exactly sane.

On the second day in the cell, one of the naked ladies heard the guards coming and said, "Oh, yay, time for our daily raping."

A daily raping? As I trembled and held myself in a ball, the naked ladies cackled. The more I cried, the more snot that bubbled from my nostrils, the more they laughed like a pair of wicked hyenas. They were speaking prison language. "Raping" meant it was time for the guards to do their daily search of our cell. I don't know what the guards thought we could've gotten our hands on; we sat there with nothing to do. We weren't allowed to go to the canteen or commissary. We couldn't have a razor to shave. We didn't even have a mattress to sleep on. We had to eat our delivered meals with cardboard spoons and forks, not that I wanted to eat much. You can't spit away the taste of cardboard from your mouth. With each daily cell search, the guards seemed like they hoped they'd find something off-limits, or in prison talk, "contraband." I felt violated and subhuman. And on top of being demoralized, nobody explained to me why I was being treated as a deplorable. With every search, I wondered, *How do they think we can manage to get ourselves a razor, a fork, a tampon from outside?*

I had a lot to learn about prison life.

Roommates came and went. I never knew what the next naked lady would do. Would this one be like the naked lady who howled at the moon all night, even though we only had two slivers in the wall they called windows? Would this one be like the naked lady who had detailed and intense conversations with the wall? Or would this one be like the naked lady who hit her head and mumbled to herself in cuss words? Oh, how I wished I had all three back again. Because this one liked to play in her own poop.

Let me back up and explain that when you are under this type of watch, you don't leave the cell. There isn't even one hour of rec time in a yard. We only were allowed one ten-minute phone call a day and one shower. So, pretty much all day long, I was forced to watch my naked roommate delight in her excrement. As if it were Play-Doh, y'all.

Sometimes she'd leave her feces in the toilet and poke at it like it was a bobblehead. One time I had to bribe her to stop, promising I don't remember what, because the stench made me hurl. She didn't shower and her skin folded, trapping sweat and bacteria and her own shit. I'm not telling you this to make you sick. I'm telling you this because I noticed she was being heavily medicated, and the whole scene, upon reflection, was unjust. Some of these people were so far gone, it was hard to believe they were cognizant enough to commit any crime. Were they just being pulled from the streets and housed at the jail? This roommate's meds would make her sleep a lot, waking only for meals, which she'd gorge herself on, and have several bowel movements. Playing with them seemed to bring her joy.

I was horrified, confused, and trapped like this for four months.

For a few days, I wondered if I should put my smock to use. I looked closely on the walls, around the bunk beds, on the ceiling, for high enough places I could tie it to.

My dad and Kristy came to visit me about a week after I had been extradited from Wisconsin. They, along with Aunt Celeste and Grandma Sharon, came from New Orleans to Springfield to see me for the first time in years. I was so nervous when I was being escorted to the visiting room, where I saw four unfamiliar faces behind glass. I didn't remember the last time I saw any of them, and as I walked toward them in handcuffs, they looked at me quizzically, as if to say, *Who is this girl?* I remember similarly thinking, *I don't know these people, but I need people right now. I need support.*

My ability to walk was the elephant in the room. I felt shy about letting them see me walk—ashamed, as if each step represented a lie I told at their expense. I didn't realize they were happy and sad at the same time. Happy that I was walking and healthy. Sad, because I didn't feel I could go to them for help. There was so much for all of us to unpack and process. We didn't understand almost 100 percent of what Mike, my attorney, reported to us. It was too fantastic to reason. As Mike uncovered medical lie after medical lie, the discovery process threw us into cognitive dissonance. Each reveal fired at us like machine-gun rounds, facts that shot at the heart.

Grandma Sharon spoke first. "How're you doing in there?"

There was no way I was going to tell them about suicide watch or the naked ladies or how shitty I felt from not having my pain meds.

"I'm okay. You know."

Good, good. Yeah, great. Fine, swell. Traffic. The small talk was killing me. I had limited time, and I needed to know . . . "What happened to Mama? Did she have a funeral? Did you go?"

My dad sat there, his face full of dread. Kristy pulled her shoulders back and said, "There was no money for a funeral, Baby. Dee Dee was cremated."

To save the ashes from being discarded, Mama's sister, Aunt Claudia, had paid for the ashes to be sent to her. I hated me. I had taken life from my mother, and now I had taken her wish for death. I thought about the smock.

As much as I thought about killing myself, I had the chance at County to be baptized for the seventh time in my life. My mother experimented with different churches and Christian denominations, so we were baptized a lot. Each time felt like a hopeful renewal and a cleansing, so I didn't mind the redundancy. But after the whole thing went down with Dan, I'd become angry at God for leaving me with her, for not showing me the way out. I'd ask God in church and before bed and in my head, over and over, *God, make this tormenting hell stop. Please help.* Nothing ever changed. I prayed to him at doctors' appointments, before procedures, when Mama put a spell on me. Two weeks before the murder, I prayed to him again. *Please don't let her make me get that surgery. Don't let them take my voice.* No one ever came. With each prayer, things only seemed to get worse, so I gave up on God.

At County, after hearing about my mother's cremation, my soul turned to ash. I felt so dirty, so unclean. I craved holy water to absorb into my skin and absolve me from my sin.

Finally, around Halloween time, I was cleared to join the general prison population, again without any explanation. To this day,

I can only speculate that the people in charge didn't see any symptoms of disease. I had been, however, having debilitating withdrawal from the oxy. Could that have been what they were doing? Detoxing me?

Coming off drugs cold turkey is not for the faint of heart, but if you are reading this and have an addiction, I plead with you to get help, because it *can* be done. The suffering of withdrawal is worth the life you will get back.

Did they observe me as I winced through stomach cramps and flu-like symptoms? In just a smock, the cold shakes, the simultaneous vomiting and diarrhea were incessant, and I had nothing to alleviate my severe discomfort. Did they not see I needed a blanket? Abandoned and without information, this was a low point for me, as I wasn't quite processing my crime and arrest. My mind just went to my mother. And back to the smock.

There were other people I missed, like Aunt Rachel, one of my mother's only true friends. We met Rachel Miller around 2007. She worked at the American Cancer Society Hope Lodge in Kansas City, where Mama and I would stay whenever I would have hospital appointments. Aunt Rachel and her family would come and visit us. We rarely had visitors, so I remember these moments vividly. They were happy times. I remember one year Aunt Rachel and her husband planned an Easter egg hunt for her kids and me. It was one of the very few holidays I had celebrated with other people. Mama trusted Aunt Rachel so much, I believe she wanted to give her power of attorney upon her death, so Rachel would be able to take care of me when Mama was gone. Mama trusted no one with me, so Rachel Miller is something special.

I spent a lot of time wondering about our friends and family, sick with worry about what they thought about me. Once I joined general population and was allowed a pen, my first letter was to Aunt Rachel. Two days after I mailed it, I received a letter back from the jail saying that I had confessed to the crime of murder. I remembered writing one line to Aunt Rachel that simply stated, "Yes, I have a part in this, but my part is small."

And that was it, the one sentence in a two-page letter someone in the mail room had read. The letter would be forwarded to the court. As soon as I could, I called Mike. "I think I messed up. They're taking it as a confession."

Just like my dad, Mike was cool. "Calm down," he said. "I'll look at it and we'll get through this."

I wanted to trust him, just like I wanted to trust my dad. But the one person I had put all my trust in had lied to me and used me for my whole life. If my own mother could hurt me and not have my back, why would Mike or my dad be any different? At first, I didn't believe Mike was trying to help me, especially when he was questioning me about things I just couldn't understand or was hearing for the first time, like that I didn't have leukemia or anemia or any of the illnesses that had defined me and confined me.

One of the other inmates at County saw how much I was struggling with the truth, with my guilt, with my loneliness, and she told me I could trust her with my feelings. It felt so damn good to just let every emotion pour out of me. At the time, waiting for trial, I was still desperately holding on to my love for Nick, missing my mother, and scared to be alone with so many strangers. The shame and guilt were like two lumps in my throat, making it so hard to talk through what I had done. And this inmate was sharing so much of her story with me, telling me she understood what I was going through. Her being vulnerable with me helped me see she was a trustworthy friend. So the ease with which I cried it out with this inmate was a lesson in why we need other people in our lives. You just can't struggle or succeed alone. We are wired not to. My wiring had been haywire for so long, so I decided she was bonding with me and it was safe to form a trust.

And then that inmate went to her public defender and told him everything I had told her in confidence.

I remember Mike coming to see me and telling me that the inmate I'd opened up to was trying to trade my "secrets," which didn't even have much to do with the crime, for a plea deal. She had used me for her own benefit. I had made myself a target of manipulation. Again.

The holy water was just a stopgap. After I learned about my mother's cremation, I began to have nightmares as my subconscious processed what had actually happened. One recurring dream was Mike, my dad, Kristy, and I rummaging through Mama's hoarding in order to clean out the house. Mike finds Mama's baby pillow in a pillow in a pillow and hands it to me, dripping with her blood. The nightmares consumed me, and I wished for oxy to take me away.

During the day, I was living in a detached dream state. I cried at night often, telling other inmates, "I miss my mom." Some would suck their teeth or act baffled, but most of them gave me a listening ear and a shoulder to cry on. Until that one inmate snitched on me to her lawyer, I remember thinking, *This is what having a friend must feel like.* In that way, I preferred jail to the isolation I felt on Volunteer Way.

In our next meeting Mike warned me not to talk to anyone anymore.

I was more alone than I had ever been, potentially digging a deeper hole for myself as we awaited my trial. I needed something bigger than myself to call upon. And so, for the first time in a very long time, I made praying a part of my daily life.

My prayer sounded more like a desperate begging: "PLEASE, GOD. Please help me. I'm so scared, God. I don't know what to do. I don't know what is happening. Why is this happening? PLEASE, God, I'm so sorry; please send me a blessing."

Giving testimony during my deposition is when I heard how Nick had so violently cut my mother. My dad and Kristy tried to protect me as much as possible from the details. They trickled information to me so I could handle it over time. It was already enough to learn that my mother had Munchausen by proxy and that my dad had not been a deadbeat after all; there was no way I could live through seeing the photos. I still haven't seen them. But I'd imagine visuals from the prosecution's cross-examination: "So, you didn't ask Nick to cut the back of her neck so deep it was down to the bone? Or stab her seventeen times?"

By the time the one-year anniversary of my mother's death came around, I was still lingering in the overcrowded jail. I found it impossible to navigate my emotions, mostly because I didn't understand them. Being shielded from the gradual process of growing up and maturing, I was now experiencing a crash course in coping.

You can't tell days from weeks in jail. Sleep folds into wakefulness. What you dream becomes shadows that walk beside you throughout the day. The first six months at County were an emotional overload. Death. Discovery. Defense. That was only the beginning. In October 2015, after I was released from suicide watch, I had my feeding tube removed by a disinterested, robotic county surgeon. When he popped it out, I was stunned at how easily I went on with my life. My mother had told me if it were ever to be removed, I'd die.

I had already gained about ten pounds, which according to Mike was an indication of how malnourished I was. County is not exactly known for its buffets, and Mike told me inmates typically lose weight upon incarceration.

I hated that damn feeding tube. It represented her absolute control over me; however, the gaping hole left behind became smaller and smaller, the healing process had begun. I constantly grazed my hand over the bandage and then the scar, like you do stitches or a new piercing. I could hear my mother's voice: "Stop fussin' with it."

Physically, my body was growing into itself, playing catch-up. I was morphing into the person that my DNA had intended. I learned my hair was brown, like I imagined. And wavy, as it began to grow in. As I put on weight, my breasts and butt rounded out. My leg muscles got stronger simply from the short walks I'd take to the canteen.

Emotionally, though, I was lost. I still grieved my mother. I missed her. She had been my only companion. I'd beat myself up for having the audacity to think such things. The hypocrisy. But the roller coaster continued, as Mike showed me the egregious medical records, and my grief would turn to anger and righteous indignation.

Every day brought a different emotion, until the first anniversary of my mother's death came around and knocked me over like a sneaky undertow. I was flattened out by the thought of what I had been doing and with whom just one year prior. All I wanted to do was escape. Escape in the opioids my cellmate had access to.

That's exactly what I did as I waited for a trial.

And then, in July 2016, God answered my prayers and sent me the blessing I had asked for. County Prosecutor Dan Patterson announced he would not seek the death penalty for either me or Nick, calling the case "extraordinary and unusual." Patterson also took into account my abuse, marked by my noticeable malnourishment, and agreed to allow me to plead guilty to a lesser crime of second-degree murder. Because of the plea deal, I didn't have to stand trial. The judge sentenced me to prison for ten years, eligible for parole in December 2023.

I didn't know it yet, but the next decade would help me get my life back.

EIGHTEEN

Qui N'Avance Pas, Recule

Who does not move forward recedes.

Compared to Greene County Jail, Chillicothe felt like a playground. Chillicothe wasn't overcrowded and filthy, and I was no longer alone. I lived in a pod that looks more like a dormitory (so I'm told)—with a key to a door and roommates. At Chillicothe, it was actually the first time I could explore.

I was freer in prison than I ever had been my whole life living with my mother. I found myself frolicking in nature more than I ever could in a wheelchair watching butterflies and slugs on Volunteer Way. A patch of grass on the side of a concrete courtyard opened my imagination. I was Fräulein Maria twirling on a hill; I was a Southern belle picking dandelions and fighting off Civil War suitors; I was Snow White yodeling to the forest creatures.

I thought about my mother a lot, reflecting on the few happy memories from my early childhood. Outside in my prison playground, I'd remember Frosty the Mardi Gras Snowman and the arts and crafts we'd do. I'd still have frequent nightmares. One recurring nightmare I began to have was of me being asleep, lying on my back in my bunk in the dark, and I'd feel something on my chest. In the nightmare I woke up to a dark figure tearing open my chest and eating my heart. When I woke up from the nightmare, I was in the same position I had been in the dream. I'd feel paralyzed and frightened with the lights off. When I'd close my eyes, the scene from the nightmare reappeared in my awake state. The demon was there. When I'd open my eyes, it would disappear.

Life at Chillicothe had its ups and downs. Points of progress and regression. I had gotten clean while at County—progress. But then the roommate I had in 2018 was still in her addiction, and upon getting her fix of Suboxone, a medication ironically intended to treat opioid addiction, she shared it with me and I relapsed. Who knew you could get addicted to the drug that's supposed to lead you out of addiction? I began to abuse Suboxone—regression.

There's definitely a pipeline in prison that makes it easy to figure out who has access to drugs. Some women got them smuggled in; sometimes guards delivered them. Other times, visitors passed them off to an inmate. All I had to say was "I have money," and the dealer would find me and supply me with Suboxone. Buying and selling drugs in prison was risky, as you can get tossed in the hole, which is prison talk for segregation, which is PC talk for solitary confinement. But when you're addicted, there are no limits to what you'll do to score.

Despite my addiction and shame, prison life was still an open field of eye-opening experiences. Wherever I turned I heard and saw things I never imagined existed. I took up smoking cigarettes and heard so much profanity and horror stories of other women's lives. I saw sex in open places.

"Have you ever had a woman go down on you?" one horny woman asked.

"I never had anything like that from anyone," was basically my answer in between nervous giggles.

"Want to try?"

Then she told me if I let her, she'd give me her serving of biscuits and gravy.

"Okay."

I was no longer in contact with Nick, but once in a while Mike would update me on the details of his trial and the seriousness of his possible sentencing. Nick ultimately received life without parole plus twenty-five years for armed criminal action. Hearing this made me feel similar to when I heard about my mother's cremation. I didn't love Nick anymore, but I knew the reason he was in this situation was partly because of how he felt about me.

One of the many positive things about my time at Chillicothe is a mandatory class I took in 2018. The class was called Impact of Crime on Victims Class, or ICVC for short. The purpose of the class is to raise awareness of the far-reaching consequences of your crime, and how your actions impacted the victims. The class was extremely powerful because it was an environment where I could begin to learn to process my past, take accountability for my crime, and understand that my mother was not the only victim of my horrible decision. One of our very first assignments was to write a letter to the person we committed a crime against. While writing it, I remembered all the people in our lives—my mother's siblings, our neighbors who loved and cared for us, and Nick. All people who were either by blood or by choice taken in by my mother's con act that hurt so many. I hadn't thought of Nick as a victim before taking this class. While he made the conscious choice to kill my mother, and do so violently, he did lose his freedom and therefore his life because I was a catalyst.

The letter I wrote to my mother gave me a peace that no holy water ever could. I had found my voice, and used it to offer my heart and soul to her, finally. I trusted God would deliver her the message and she would forgive me for what I had done.

Mother,

I am now twenty-eight years old and in prison for my part in your murder, and although I can never justify my crime, nor can any letter or apology give back the life that was taken, I am writing this as if you were physically in front of me to express all that I have held in for the whole of my life.

I am writing this letter having had nearly five years to feel the emotions felt when expressing the words written. Every day since your death, I have had nothing but time to reflect on the choices that have led me to where I am today, moreover of how your own actions formed the circumstances around mine. The woman writing this letter to you is far different than the girl who was once broken and desperate to live what I would later come to understand as just an average life for a young woman. Living twenty-three years of my life with you as my only guardian, the one person who had the responsibility of shaping who I would grow up to become. Unfortunately, my upbringing was a far cry from that which it should have been.

Starting from my birth going into my young adulthood, being isolated from having any other human interaction other than with you was lonely, and has affected my ability to have appropriate social skills necessary to make healthy social interaction with others.

The many unnecessary medical surgical procedures and medications that were forced on me, to "treat" illnesses that I did not have, left my body marked with scars both physical and emotional.

Your choice to not have me educated growing up has made it difficult to gain the appropriate level of education needed for a woman of my age, and has caused a depleted self-esteem in my ability to make achievements in society.

When mentioning the overall lack of life experience that was withheld from me by your choice as my mother, you not only took away the normal experiences that shape an individual to be who they are, or could be, but you made the choice to keep me from the best things in life that make life worth living as a youth. The innocent joy of having a first day of school. The fun of going to the mall with friends and buying a dress that would surely never pass your approval. The excitement of being asked to prom. The comfort of your embrace when getting my heart broken for the first time. The nerves of awaiting that college acceptance letter.

These are all things that I was not able to experience.

It would be many years before I was able to fully understand the reasons why I grew up being isolated from others, being taken to hospital after hospital, doctor after doctor, without anything being medically wrong with me. Waiting for the next time your hand was to strike me for simply trying to make a friend. Fear, manipulation, and isolation were all I knew of your kind of "love," and the lingering question of why I was unable to be allowed the one thing that everyone else seemed to have—the ability of free will.

Mom, after all that has happened, I have been searching for answers and spending my time trying to learn about myself as a person, trying to make sense of why all these events unfolded with this amount of tragedy. I want you to know that I now understand that you were mentally and emotionally unstable when raising me, and that your actions were the result of a disorder called "Munchausen by proxy" that creates abuse inflicted on a child due to mental illness of the parent.

With now having the answers I sought to find, I am able to finally let go of the resentment I held against you and forgive you, and moreover I want to let you know that I'm so sorry for having a part in your death—murder was never the answer or solution. There is not a single day that you go unremembered, and I will carry this regret and remorse for the rest of my life. I will always love you for bringing me into this world, and will remember you with love for the woman I know was a good person behind the mental disorder.

Going forward, I will take my past and turn it from pain to perseverance, advocating for children who have suffered abuse at the hands of a parent, sharing my story with others to spread awareness of what Munchausen by proxy is and the ways people can recognize the warning signs, in the hopes that I can educate and make the next child who wonders "why is Mommy doing this to me?" that much braver to reach out for help, telling a listening ear before he or she is behind bars for thinking murder is a way out.

I can never undo the hurt that was caused by my actions, but I hope by doing this, I am remembering you well, and making a positive difference with your memory.

I love you, Mom.

Gypsy-Rose Blanchard
2018, Chillicothe Correctional Center, Missouri

I felt this was so helpful that I signed up for multiple twelve-week-long classes. I received certificates of completion, which still are valuable reminders of my search for understanding. At one point, I was taking four classes at one time. Learning was so much fun; it made me sad that I hadn't had a chance to be a formal student. I was even able to facilitate ICVC and a class called Pathways to Change. For the ICVC class, I needed to be trained to teach, which was really rewarding. This is where I fell in love with the idea of mentoring others.

According to the penal system, I didn't qualify for formal psychotherapy, which was ironic, being that my first stop at Greene County was suicide watch. I was too "well." For a person who was always told she wasn't ever well, this was surprising to hear. However, I was able to read books on a bunch of issues that definitely affected me: codependency, PTSD, insecurity, abandonment, personality disorders, addiction, trust, and on and on. Books were a salvation. Sadly, toward the end of my time at Chillicothe, books were banned; they were being used to traffic drugs into the prison. Knowing how much books help, labeling them contraband seemed like a drastic measure that would render itself ineffective in the long run. Where there's a will, there's a way.

One very impactful course I took was on codependency. I read about attachment, and learned how and why we form attachments, especially dysfunctional ones. Attachment styles usually begin with the mother. I learned that my attachment to my mother was an insecure one, so I made it my mission to please her on the off chance I could turn some of her other personalities in my favor. My self-worth was dictated by what my mother thought of me, how she reacted to my performances, and the big one: whether or not she'd withhold her love. Love was a dangling carrot that made me jump higher to please her, even if it meant going against what felt right.

My brain had felt like a tossed salad for so long, and now insight and knowledge were available to me if I wanted them. I went on a personal quest to discover who I was without my mother, without being judged by my crime. Where other inmates saw confinement, I saw opportunities to learn independence. I even got a job as a janitor. I mopped the floors of the dining room before and after my thirty-minute lunch break, I Windexed fingerprints off the plexiglass shields on the sides of pay phones, and I removed crumpled balls of tissues from the visitors' room. Sometimes I worked outside in the yard, where I disposed of cigarette butts, fresh wads of gum, and general debris blowing around. For some, that might feel confining, but the prison yard was like a playground to me.

Aside from having a job, I was responsible for my own space and had to navigate how to live with other people, how to make friends—or not. *Who am I? What makes me tick?* I didn't know any-thing at all. I didn't even know what size clothing I was, because I was always dressed in some costume or boys' clothes. The only times I wore a pair of jeans—that were hand-me-downs—were the night I tried to run off with Dan and when I left the house with Nick after the murder.

I didn't know what shoe size I was until I bought my first pair, on the day of my release from Chillicothe. You wear booties in jail, not shoes.

After a lifetime of spending most of my days sitting around watching television, waiting for a doctor's appointment or an errand to run, my routine at Chillicothe initially made me feel busy. As much as I am not a morning person, I liked having somewhere to be, even when somewhere was absolutely nowhere. All that mattered was living out my day with nobody holding my hand. Without my mother's restrictions, my days felt fuller and freer.

The one thing that was similar to the life I lived with my mother was living by a schedule, except my mother's schedule was set by a timer for medication dosages. But in a way that familiarity helped with the transition.

7:30 A.M. Count time. We sat up in our bunks and turned the lights on. Corrections officers (COs for short) accounted for all inmates. This took about fifteen to twenty minutes, after which I went back to sleep.

10:30 A.M. Got down from my top bunk, clicked on my TV, made a cup of instant coffee. With my coffee in hand, I headed to the dayroom. Sometimes I'd make phone calls, but they were really short before I earned time and privileges. Then I'd go back to my room, look at my locker, pick from my canteen items, make mac and cheese or some other processed packaged food, like ramen noodles, and go back to the dayroom.

1:30–3 P.M. We'd have recreation time. I liked to work out on the elliptical machine for about an hour. I'd come back to the housing unit, shower, and by the time I was out and dressed, it was around 3 P.M.

3 P.M. I went to work. I took out the trash, swept and mopped, changed toilet paper rolls, and so on.

4:30 P.M. Count time again. We returned to our rooms and sat on our bunks until the COs finished.

5–10 P.M. Free time for phone use or other things, like reading or playing games or studying. I was able to get my GED while at Chillicothe.

10 P.M. Count time and time for bed.

How do you go about figuring out who you are when you spent your life unconsciously playing pretend? Like everyone else doing life, I had to cycle through a ton of growing phases. Trial and error over and over.

In many ways, I went through adolescence in prison. And since prison is like a grown-up high school—women in their forties act like they're sixteen—the environment was perfect. When I first got there, I joined a clique and I tried to be one of the mean girls. I took on a new nickname—Jersey—because I acted like my shit don't stink, like I was a Mafia girl in *The Sopranos* or something. But a girl from the Bayou can't imitate the Meadowlands. Plus, my idea of a mean girl/Jersey persona meant I had to make fun of people or act judgy, like, "Oh my God, did you see what she was doing in the

179

canteen?" It's not nice to make fun of people, and I realized quickly that I wasn't a mean girl.

Then, I went through a goth phase and listened to heavy metal and wore black lipstick. That was brief too. Did the tomboy thing, which was only defined by my short hair at the time. I kept trying on different hats and different friend groups to see which one fit, just like any adolescent is expected to do, except I was in my twenties.

I tried to experiment with my sexuality too. I was pretty sure I was straight, but I tried anyway. Because of sexual abuse I had experienced, and the way my mother made me feel dirty in my own womanly body, I had a mental block that prevented me from full satisfaction. I thought perhaps if I experimented with women, I would have a better chance of reaching climax. I think as a young girl I was exposed to watching shows like *Xena: Warrior Princess*— Xena and Gabrielle were lesbians—and I watched it and didn't understand it. When I was around sixteen, I thought girls were pretty, and that confused me, so I thought: *Am I gay?* There's a saying in prison, "Gay for the stay, straight from the gate," so when in Rome . . . I did kiss a couple girls and became a pillow princess, four times. (That's when you receive instead of give.) Nothing ever "happened" down there, so I figured I was straight.

I was trying to bloom and grow. Chillicothe was my greenhouse: not exactly a natural habitat, but good enough to get the job done. In order to bloom, an old part of myself had to wither away.

The guilt and the shame that defined me had to be reconciled. The trial and error and experimenting with my persona and testing my interests helped me chisel away the old insecure self that had been a Frankenstein of my mother's making. The more I learned about what I wanted and needed, the more confident I became in who I was, what I was capable of doing, and the potential I had to go further. The more I learned about self-worth and forgiveness—of myself and others—the more I began to trust my judgment of people, trust that I could tell the difference between friends and foes.

Growing up friendless, I had no idea what to expect of a friend or how to be one, other than what I learned from actresses like Miley Cyrus and Selena Gomez on Disney Channel shows. I didn't know there were different categories or levels of friendship, that acquaintances play a different role than friends, or what an inner circle was or how to build one. Other than Aunt Rachel, my mother didn't model friendship for me with a group of Golden Girls or besties from high school. What is a true friend? What is a fake friend? I had no idea. But I really wanted one. There's another prison motto: "You don't come to prison to make friends."

How do you make friends in a friendless environment? You take a chance.

When I met Lori and Amelia, I realized what a good friend was. Each of them had been my roommate at one time. Neither befriended me out of fascination with my infamy; it happened organically, a blossoming. Before I met Lori and Amelia, I felt

181

like I was giving so much to my prison relationships. Always listening and giving, and one day I realized I wasn't getting anything back from these people. But true friends, I now know, make you a better person, and Lori and Amelia did that and then some. I found my tribe. There is nothing more meaningful than knowing you found your people. Having a feeling of belonging changes a life.

But first you have to feel.

Numbing myself with Suboxone was not the answer. For a million reasons, I needed to stop. The main reason I had turned to painkillers in the first place was to leave my world behind. Now, to heal, I needed to be present, not vacant. I was so afraid of the withdrawals. They were brutal back at County. Could I go through them again? Then, I hit, as they say, my rock bottom. I lied to Kristy and asked her for fifty dollars because I told her I broke this girl's CD player and needed cash to reimburse the girl. Kristy trusted me and I hurt that trust. I used the money to buy drugs. I told Kristy how sorry I was, that it wasn't right I hurt that trust. She said, "I forgive you. I love you all the same."

Her forgiveness surprised me. It gave me the courage to quit. Cold turkey. I told myself that this time around, at least I knew what to expect. Facing my demons had to be done sober.

Without the numbing, my life was beginning to change. I was beginning to feel like someone worthy of giving love and receiving it, who was even happy. I had found acceptance and love with trusted friends and family. My relationship with Dad and Kristy had flourished through constant phone calls, frequent letter writing, and their own in-person visits where they'd bring me homemade food and pictures and tell me stories about my early life, memories that were never mine before.

For every story my mother had told me about my dad, Kristy, and my siblings, Dad had an alternate version. In the beginning, our visits together were like first dates, until I felt comfortable enough to ask Dad and Kristy questions about some of the moments of disappointment I remembered.

Mike Stanfield was the one who first told me that my father had been sending money and letters and gifts for me all those years. I didn't believe him.

"I sent you cards for every occasion," Dad said.

"But she told me you didn't even know when my birthday was."

"I sent you a laptop one year, didn't you get it?"

"But she told me we got that from charity."

"I left messages on your mama's voicemail wondering about you and wanting to know if she got the money I sent for the operation."

"But she told me you didn't care about me; that you were all about having a son, and now that you got one, I was dead to you."

"Do you know how many times I called Dee Dee to try to plan trips with you?" Kristy said. "I even wanted to take you for long holidays."

"But she told me that you were a bitch and that Dad was beating you and you deserved it."

"She always thought we were cheating behind her back, and that wasn't true," Kristy said.

Dad and Kristy wanted me. They loved me. You would think such news would've elated me. Instead, I felt sadder than I ever had, like I was back in the shed, awaking from the dream I had of our happy life.

NINETEEN

Amour Amour

My public life really began when my family and I participated in the HBO documentary *Mommy Dead and Dearest*, which aired in May 2017. An independent documentary filmmaker named Erin Lee Carr contacted Dad, Kristy, and Mike about doing a documentary about my childhood and interviewing me. There had been so much press coverage surrounding Nick and me, it felt good to have an opportunity to explain my side of the story. They began production as I was awaiting my court hearing, before the plea deal. But I remember vividly that I was interviewed hours after I accepted the plea.

In the process, I learned so much about what my dad and Kristy had gone through, too, and hearing from extended family members was enlightening. It helped provide a context to see how far-reaching my mother's impact had been.

None of us expected the response. While, yes, there were haters, the outpouring of support was shocking. People from all over the world sent me letters of encouragement, support, and of their own stories. My story opened a floodgate for other people's pain and, I think, their hope that they, too, can survive. My heart broke as I read letters depicting graphic abuse, hopelessness, and shame. Family members of imprisoned loved ones wrote to my dad and Kristy, looking for connection in a club they did not choose to be in.

One letter in particular stuck out to me. His voice leaped off the page, as if he were sitting right in front of me. Holding the paper, I could feel his energy. He was just a cool guy. "Hi, my name is Ken."

Ken. Funny. My mother never liked Barbie's Ken. *Fuck it,* I thought. I wrote him back.

We wrote each other letters and started talking on the phone. He was easy to talk to, and we had so much in common. He was from a big family with lots of siblings, which, having been brought up as an only child, appealed to me. I imagined their holiday gatherings being really loud and chaotic, and that brought on a smile. I couldn't wait for Ken to visit me. When he did, I was swept off my feet. *Dang, he's handsome.* After thirty-seven minutes, he leaned over and gave me the most passionate kiss of my whole life.

"I didn't even know you liked me like that," I said, as the guard charged toward us. "Yeah, I have for a while," he said.

"I have for a while too."

Poor Ken got kicked out for that kiss since the rule is "NO TOUCHING." I got lucky, because that's an offense that can get you thrown in the hole. It was 100 percent worth it. The first time Ken told me he loved me felt like I had taken the most powerful opioid of all. Love was my new drug.

"Will you be my husband one day?" I asked him on the phone, after about a year of our friendship and courtship.

"Of course," he said. And while I hadn't proposed, his confirming that his plans for us would one day be mutual had me walking on air.

During an October visit, about a year after that call, disregarding the rules, Ken held my hands close and told me how much I meant to him. I had had a feeling a proposal was coming, since we'd talked about our future together, but I never expected such beautiful words like the ones Ken spoke to me in the visitor's room:

"Gypsy, I know you through and through and I love you for who you are today, for the heart I've come to know." Then Ken motioned his hands over his chest, over his heart, and continued, "I want to spend every day waking up next to you, building a life with you, and being the one that you can come to through all the hard times. I want to be that one for you. Will you marry me?"

"Yes."

He couldn't propose with a ring because of prison restrictions on bringing offenders gifts. I did find a silver band for sale on the black market in prison. An inmate was getting a divorce and was selling her silver band, so I bought it. It was confiscated shortly after.

We kept our engagement private, only telling our closest family. Then *The Act* aired on Hulu, and I went from being "known" to a being pseudocelebrity. My personal life was a carcass for vultures to feast on. The media, including true crime armchair enthusiasts, investigated everything about me, including Ken. The invasion was really hard on him.

After an acquaintance of one of my family members leaked my relationship, clickbait articles appeared mockingly announcing our engagement. Ken was a private person and was bothered by the attention and scrutiny. The news of our engagement reached Nick, who sent me a letter in 2019, not too long after he got sentenced.

Basically Nick said I was committing adultery. That he had taken my virginity (when he raped me), and that by God's law, we were married. The letter was reminiscent of his dominant role that he was obsessed with playing out when we had our internet relationship. His attempt to control me and humiliate me as his submissive for his own deviant sexual pleasure had gotten old. Only because I was in a healthy relationship with Ken, who was my best friend, who made me feel special and appreciated, was I finally able to see how pathological Nick and I were when we were together.

I wrote him one letter back, which acted as a closure letter. Codefendants in the state of Missouri can communicate and even be housed together, but becoming pen pals (no pun intended) was never my intention. In the letter to Nick, I told him I didn't want to get back into a relationship with him. That I'd moved on. I covered everything I wanted him to know, from A to Z, from getting arrested all the way to the present, about how I felt. How we were basically children, adults with mindsets of children, going through this ordeal. I told him I realized he didn't have much outside experience and I understood that, and I felt a sense of guilt, which is why I testified on his behalf at his trial. I felt that taking accountability for my role was the right thing to do. I didn't do it out of love but out of a sense of obligation and due diligence to justice.

I needed to make sure I was clear on that, because I didn't want Nick to misconstrue my letter for wanting to be with him.

I thought at first that it was Ken's discomfort with the popularity of *The Act* and the widening of my reputation that led him to end our relationship. I was wrong. At the time of this writing, Ken has reached out to explain and set the record straight. There were many adults in his life, presumably much "wiser" than he, who suggested it wasn't the right time for me to be married. "If you love her, you'll set her free," was the common piece of advice he'd hear again and again, sometimes from prominent Hollywood therapists and other media personalities—sometimes from those in my own immediate family. I see now, he believed he was acting in my best interest by sacrificing his own needs and wants.

The rite of passage of losing my first love happened alone in prison instead of in my bedroom, surrounded by girlfriends playing me a breakup mix and us eating pints of Ben & Jerry's, like in the movies. It was a time when I missed my mom, a time that should've been shared between a mother and a daughter but never would be.

I thought about drugs. I thought about the smock. Instead, I cut off all my hair and made depression my new friend. My faith, along with the passing of time and lots of crying to Kristy, revealed that God had a plan for me—another blessing.

He had seen the very same documentary on HBO that Ken had, but Ryan Anderson didn't write me until much later.

Ryan came into my life during a time when I had hardened my heart. Rebound? Maybe. I couldn't see that then. He was very charming. His deep voice and familiar Southern accent made me feel safe and special. Having grown up in Louisiana, Ryan felt like home to me, because Ryan was also a proud Louisianian. We bantered about his favorite football team, the New Orleans Saints, and mine, the Kansas City Chiefs. I could learn to love the Saints, I'd say all flirty on the phone. I had lived in Louisiana *and* Missouri, after all.

But I didn't want to trust again. There was that choice once more; I was still stuck. My fear and feeling that I wasn't good enough were like brick walls that I couldn't bust through. Do I let Ryan in? Do I try this again and risk getting hurt?

Ryan's sense of humor lifted my vibrations—and he laughed at my jokes too. Soon I was growing impatient for our next phone call. We had deep conversations about life, about pop culture, about our hopes for the future. He shared with me his fears and vulnerabilities and his Kryptonite. In return, I spilled every dark moment I had growing up. Ryan was the only person I had been able to, finally, open up to and not feel ashamed for my actions and past. We prayed together. We planned together. Some say he was my distraction, and he afforded me something happy to look forward to day after day. Even though Ryan wasn't in prison, I think I was the same for him.

Ryan and I fought, too, like any old regular couple. And I think those arguments made our relationship deeper and more serious. I showed my ugly side to Ryan. You know, like that point in a new relationship when you fart or leave the bathroom door open? I worked out a lot of shit with him, tossing him my baggage. I'd feel bad, after the fact, about doing that. But then he'd toss me his baggage and I'd say, "Oh, okay, we're doing this."

Ryan learned my triggers and I his. Once he told me, "You're my heart," and my body felt like it was trapped in a room filling up with water, so I cussed him out.

He didn't know my mother had said that to me constantly.

It's inevitable that the things that my mother did and said, and how I was raised, will affect certain decisions and behaviors moving forward, but I don't want them to. I want clarity on how I live and what I choose to carve out for myself and my future family. That will take work—but I'm a hard worker. I've been working on this ever since my release from prison.

Ryan and I talked multiple times throughout the day and for hours before bed. This enabled us to fast-track our relationship until we finally made our marriage commitment to each other. Many people, including my dad and Kristy, told me not to marry Ryan. It was obvious Ken had never left my heart. They at least wanted us to wait, but I see now that after a lifetime of being in love with the idea of being in love, in my thirties I felt this desperate need to find and create a family that I was once robbed of, complete with a Southern Prince Charming. Even if it wasn't meant to be.

In October of 2022, about four months after Ryan and I had our prison wedding, the weight of the responsibility of being someone's wife hit me hard. Self-doubt smeared my fledgling self-worth, and being Mrs. Anderson threw a wrench in my still-developing identity.

Friends and family were skeptical and concerned, so there were lots of cooks in the kitchen, turning up the flame. But also, I was afraid to be accountable to someone again. The relationships I had with my mother and with Nick required me to be bossed around. As a teacher, Ryan's natural demeanor was to take charge, and that personality trait seemed to rattle me, reminding me of how I was raised. Alone and tired of crying over the latest argument Ryan and I had, I thought I could share my fear and confusion with some trusted friends, writing:

"Hi friends, I just want to let you know I am thinking about going forward with an annulment."

I was hoping my friends would talk me off the ledge, tell me it was normal to feel this way, that the finality of being married sinks in for so many newlyweds—and that would be that. But they didn't. They knew we weren't supposed to be together, but like every other lesson I've learned in life, I'd have to figure that out on my own.

TWENTY

Aigre-Doux

Sour-sweet

I had managed to be in prison for about six years without going to the hole. Drugs didn't get me there. Ken's passionate kiss didn't get me there. Nor did bad behavior. Of a population of roughly 2,500 at Chillicothe, it's rare to meet a woman who hasn't been in segregation. I prided myself on being one of the few. That was strategic, because unlike many inmates, I had something to lose—release. I was careful and hell-bent on letting nothing get in the way of my parole. I kept my head down and only hung around with my closest friends, Lori and Amelia. Getting involved in the business of rival groups was a surefire way to be charged with a new crime that could add time to your sentence. Hell no. If there was drama, I looked the other way. A fight? I'd slither out of the rec room.

It was September 2021. I had a little over two years until my eligible parole date of December 2023, but I had been preparing for my upcoming meeting with the parole board in December 2021. In Missouri, inmates who have completed 85 percent of their sentence fulfill the "mandatory minimum" and meet with the parole board for the first time. Ryan and I—we'd patched up our differences—began to dream out loud about the fantasy of me getting paroled early. At worst, the twenty-four months gave us a timeline to slash pen marks through.

Ryan described the apartments he was scoping out for us. Those phone calls discussing my wish list for a home made my days pass more quickly and easily. The last time I made such a wish list was for Habitat for Humanity. It was for a playhouse, a ramp, and a hot tub. My mother was the one who had the idea to paint it her favorite color, pink. My taste grew up as I did. Now, instead of a life-size Barbie Dreamhouse, I wanted granite countertops and stainless steel appliances and hardwood floors and high ceilings. And I definitely needed a patio or a terrace, somewhere I could go to get some sun and breathe fresh air whenever I pleased. That would be the best part of freedom. To be in nature.

One morning at around 10 AM, I was in my pajamas having my morning coffee, watching the Food Network, when a CO (corrections officer) appeared in the doorway.

"Miss Blanchard, I need you to come with me."

"Okay," I said, furrowing my brows.

I was really nervous as I followed him down to the rotunda where another guard stood. *Is he waiting for me?* The CO said nothing; he simply presented me to the guard, handed me over, and walked away.

"What? Wait? Is this a joke? What am I in trouble for? What did I do?" I spun my head around, as if the answers could be found in the air around me.

"I don't know," said the guard. "But I got to put the handcuffs on you."

His demeanor was neutral as he took me by the arm and walked me outside the housing unit and into a holding cell where there was another inmate sleeping. I spotted an intercom and buzzed it, unclear of who might answer.

"Yes," said the voice.

"Excuse me, ummm, why am I downstairs?"

"You're under investigation," the voice said.

"For what?" I asked, my face burning.

"We don't know."

Nobody knew anything, yet I was held there for three days until I had a committee hearing to determine my penalty for my mystery infraction.

"Do you know why you are under investigation?" the sergeant asked during the hearing. The last time somebody asked me that question, I was in a sheriff's office in Wisconsin. This time, I was telling the whole truth.

"No, not at all," I said, wiping the sweat from my palms.

"Well, we don't either," he said.

An ominous feeling came over me. I knew this feeling. It was the same feeling I had when my mother wheeled me against my will to the shed. I didn't know why I was in trouble. There was no reasoning with anyone. *I'm not in control.*

"What's happening? What's going to happen now?" I cried.

"You've been assigned to segregation."

"The hole?" I wanted to jump out of my chair and run. *What in the holy fuck? What did I even do?*

Being escorted to the hole felt like a funeral procession. Other inmates who were walking around camp had to stop walking, turn their backs to me, as I walked behind the CO. They would remain frozen like that until we passed through. My tears streamed down my khaki uniform, turning it dark brown, the color of dirt, as I moved slowly toward what felt like my final resting place. I was being buried alive and the gravediggers had no idea why. *How will Ryan and my parents know where I am? For sure they'll be worried when they don't hear from me.*

Gossip travels like wildfire in prison, but a story about the hole travels at lightning speed. My friend Lori was told by another inmate that I was taken down. She called Ryan and told him what had happened.

Without explanation, everyone's imaginations went wild. *Was Gypsy in the hole because of one of Ryan's visits? Did they kiss or touch too intimately? Could she have gone back to drugs? Did another inmate make up a story to fuck with her?*

Ryan called the prison, but they wouldn't tell him anything either. Finally, I was informed that I was put in the hole because they were investigating me for a potential plan to escape prison. "My parole hearing is in a few months and I've already done the majority of my time," I said. "I would never do that. I'm not fucking crazy, y'all!"

Being in the hole for a solid two weeks was the same as being kidnapped. I had no access to time or people. I sat there in the dark not knowing my fate or how long the punishment would be. I was defenseless. In the dark, literally and figuratively.

There was nonstop noise in the hole. Screaming was incessant. There was a women next door to me who screamed all hours of the night. Shrill noises I couldn't shake from my ears. Banging and arguing echoed throughout the day. Day and night, I was being assassinated by sounds of desperation.

To keep myself sane I envisioned the apartment Ryan was hunting for. *Maybe the bathroom will have a dressing table to put makeup on and do my hair? I should add that to my wish list.* I prayed to God a lot. "God, give me the strength to survive this. Please don't let this affect my parole." I put all my faith in God that he had gotten me this far. I thanked him for sending me his blessing when the courts showed me mercy. *I don't want to be greedy, God, but please can you send me another blessing?*

In the hole, I could only take a five-minute shower twice a week—and it's a cage shower, so you're standing under the sprinkler naked in front of the female guards. When you go into the cage shower, there is a cubbyhole for you to put your hands through, like the ones in Western movies, so guards can uncuff you from the other side. There was a toilet in my cell, so I had to do my business out in the open. The goal is to take away your dignity. Mine was flushed on day one.

For two weeks, I was reminded that I had no rights. Someone wrote on social media something like, "She doesn't belong in prison. I wish I could bust her out." An unknown source reported the post to the prison. And that was it. Authorities went through my stuff, looking for writings or plans or any correspondence that indicated I knew the person who wrote the troublemaking post. Which I didn't.

Letting me out of the hole came with as much explanation as going in. Poof, suddenly, I could go back. An inmate who rejoins population after segregation looks markedly different, weathered, like a prisoner of war failing to assimilate to their regular life. Nothing is regular again after hole time. I still have nightmares. In one dream they put me in the hole for being Wiccan. In another, male guards put me in the hole for not stripping for them on demand. In another dream I'm in a cell in the hole, and Ryan is in an adjacent cell, and we whisper to each other through the vents.

Upon returning to population, I did my best to resume my normal routine. My parole hearing was still set for December 9, but I was freaking out for two months straight that my time in the hole would tarnish my parole eligibility in December 2023.

Around nine in the morning on the day of the hearing, Kristy met me in a visitation room, where we sat with Deputy Warden Amy Parkhurst and videoconferenced in two other members of the parole board. I had asked Kristy to be my delegate to speak on my behalf. One of the men on the screen asked me questions, none of which were about the crime itself. They were interested in hearing from me personally about my upbringing and relationship with my mother. I told him a little about the abuse. He asked me where I had met Nick. He said he was not familiar with my case, at least the details of it, so I explained our story. Then he wanted to hear about the programs I participated in and completed while at Chillicothe. I showed my certificates and also my GED. I remember him saying he was proud of me. He even complimented me on only having thirteen minor infractions, which are just write-ups.

"Have you had any mental health treatment while you have been here?" Deputy Warden Parkhurst asked.

"No, ma'am. I tried, but did not qualify."

Deputy Warden Parkhurst validated the trauma I endured, and she encouraged me to seek therapy upon my release. Kristy jumped in, enthusiastically, saying, "She has loving parents and siblings and we will all get her the support she needs. Heck, we'll all go into therapy!"

Deputy Warden Parkhurst explained that it takes the board up to four weeks' time to make their decision. That was a Thursday. By the following Monday, I was called to the office of the institutional parole officer to give me my letter in person. I stood before her, took a deep breath, held it, and opened the seal.

Gypsy-Rose Blancharde
Release date: December 28, 2023

Being granted early parole, I felt like a pregnant woman waiting out the first trimester to share her news. Believe me, I wanted to shout it from the rooftops: "I'M BEING RELEASED ON DECEMBER 28, 2023, Y'ALL!" But there was too much at stake.

People in prison get jealous of short-timers. They'd call my sentence "baby time." Sometimes they even retaliate and try to get you in trouble to jeopardize parole. After going to the hole for no reason at all, I couldn't risk anyone finding out. I started eating alone, keeping to myself. I think some people suspected something was up because I'm a chatterbox by nature.

We also wanted to keep the media from finding out I was getting released two years early. After *The Act*, there was a lot of gossip. I didn't want haters to dampen the hope I had in my heart.

Ryan moved into our apartment before me, decorating it with fleur-de-lis pillows and wall art. The symbol of New Orleans, the fleur-de-lis was my mother's go-to accessory around the house and in our front yard. "There'll be no beige anywhere," Ryan said, assuring me our color scheme would be bright and happy, with gold accents everywhere. "You've seen enough beige for a lifetime."

He told me he'd tested out the kitchen, making gumbo, he joked, that rivaled my dad's. I could smell the Cajun seasoning. I could see Ryan in a silly apron that said something like *I don't need Google, I have Gypsy.* Maybe we'd even get a dog. I was letting myself go to the places in my imagination that I had been afraid to go. I was no longer afraid to let myself hope. Or trust. I thought we were skiing downhill with the wind at our backs.

Our monthly countdown whittled to weeks, and the Xs I penned on the calendar felt like kisses. My dad and Kristy and Ryan planned the logistics of my release date. I, on the other hand, was focused on what really mattered: *What will I wear?* I wanted to look pretty for Ryan, but I had never planned an outfit before. Either my mother dressed me, or I wore a khaki uniform. It was a lot of fun asking my sister, Mia, what was trendy. I had to guess my jean size, and Ryan went out and shopped for me. I still giggle at how lost he must've looked roaming around the women's department, trying to tell the difference between skinny jeans and high-rise and boot cut. I'm pretty sure he went back to exchange them three times! The real challenge was the shoes. He needed to pick out just the right pair, but also guess my shoe size. Ryan would then mail my ensemble and shoes in a "dress-out box" with my name on it, which I would change into the morning of my release.

I had an actual day. December 28, 2023. I said it over and over again, never getting sick of the sound. *Someone just pinch me please.*

Well, the joke was on me. One day in August, about four months before my release, I was in the canteen, when a bunch of inmates approached me: "We know you got parole . . ."

I tried to play dumb, but you can't outscam a bunch of scam artists.

Blindsided and angry, I called Dad and Kristy. We had managed to keep it under wraps for almost a year, until someone leaked the story to *In Touch Weekly.* It was, we think, someone Kristy had told in confidence. And it was a hard lesson, and a warning, about what we needed to do when I was released: keep our circle small.

That was going to be hard. I was trying to do two things at once: embrace my public platform and maintain an inner circle that I was 100 percent certain wouldn't screw me or the rest of my beloved family. Could these two things happen simultaneously? Yes, but not without making a LOT of mistakes along the way.

I tried to put the negativity of the snitch out of my mind. Finally, my future was the *near* future. One more holiday season to cycle through, and I'd be with Ryan on New Year's Eve. What would we do? How would we celebrate the beginning of 2024? While it felt like a tease to be released just three days after Christmas, having the week between Christmas and New Year's to celebrate my freedom worked out for friends and family who wanted to travel to Missouri to be with me. They were planning a big ole belated Christmas for me, something I never had before, with presents and food and lots of laughter and love. Oh, and one small Lifetime channel camera crew.

Kristy went into her usual take-charge mode, looking for a rental house in Overland Park, Kansas, just over the Missouri line, that would fit all of us. Her hands cramped from wrapping so many presents. And she and Mia were my personal shoppers, because I wanted to have gifts for everyone too. Kristy and Mia bought confetti, party decorations, and baked a buttercream-frosted sheet cake, complete with rainbow sprinkles and candles that spelled out "Celebrate."

When Ryan told me that the Kansas City Chiefs were playing the New Orleans Saints on New Year's Eve, I was psyched. This was a sign! The two cities I had grown up in playing on such a special night. It wasn't just a sign; it was symbolic. My dad bought us tickets for seats in the sixth row. Ryan ordered me a bunch of Chiefs swag, including a pompom ski hat, while he coordinated his own over-the-top Saints garb. The plan was to have our first New Year's kiss at Arrowhead Stadium. What better way to spend the New Year than to ring in a new life?

TWENTY-ONE

Libérée

Released

Three days away from my release date, I spent Christmas Day crying. When I wasn't crying, I slept the day away. When I wasn't sleeping, I paced. Time felt like a straitjacket.

I purposely didn't speak to Ryan or Dad and Kristy on Christmas Eve or Christmas Day. It felt intrusive to call. Dad and Kristy's house at Christmastime is usually busting at the seams. Ryan was with his own family. Something inside me told me to let them enjoy their traditions the way they were used to—without me. In just a few days, everyone's lives would be forever altered. I felt this was especially true for my brother and sister. I wanted to be sensitive to their feelings. They'd had our parents to themselves all their lives, and here comes the long-lost daughter. I imagined them at the dinner table thinking how it's the last time Christmas will be exactly this way. Were they happy or sad about that? If they were sad, I don't blame them. Change, even good change, can be sad. I think that's why I felt so down those last days.

My life also would be changing. The only friends I ever had were at Chillicothe. The only job I worked was there too. The only education I received was within those walls. When I arrived at Chillicothe, I felt freer than I ever had. Although I had outgrown that version of freedom, it was still bittersweet to leave it behind.

December 28, 2023

Typically, when inmates are released, they change into the clothes given to them in their "dress-out box." Some people file onto a bus that takes them to a bus station; others are picked up by someone they know.

I was the exception to the rule. Since the news of my parole broke, along with announcements of a docuseries Lifetime was filming, the media's interest in my release was intense. This concerned the authorities at Chillicothe; nobody wanted a scene. Ryan was going to pick me up, but we didn't know what time I'd be released until the prison called him. The secretiveness surrounding my discharge made it feel like a prison break, except with the help of the prison! The Lifetime crew and Ryan were staying minutes up the road, waiting for the call telling them when they should head over. GoPros were placed inside Ryan's car, a blatant reminder that mine was no ordinary release.

Hands shaking, I changed into my blue jeans and blue-and-white long-sleeved shirt, savoring the moment I had been praying for. I was so excited to put my black platform-heeled boots on, but they wouldn't zip up past my ankles. My white socks would have to do.

Ryan got the call at 2:30 A.M. to pick me up within forty-five minutes. He headed to the prison, followed by the film crew. Once they reached the perimeter, police barricaded the area and told the crew to leave.

The biting winter air felt exhilarating as I was escorted from the back of the prison to the passenger side of Ryan's car. I thought about the last time I was outside in the middle of the night to feel how low Missouri's temperatures can dip. I had forgotten what night air smelled like. The car door shut, and just like that, I was alone with my husband in a warm car.

There wasn't even time for a proper kiss. Ryan just pulled away as I buckled my seat belt for the most surreal ride of my life. I thought he was going so fast! I had forgotten the sensation of moving in a car; I was afraid I'd get sick. I marveled at the iPhone Ryan handed to me, like a cavewoman who traded in her sticks and rocks for a flashing, vibrating, beeping heap of plastic.

I hadn't had a full night's sleep in a week. The heat from the vents lulled me, and I felt instantly exhausted but fought off sleep until I became hyper on the short ride. I would've put toothpicks under my eyelids to not miss a beat of this moment. Ryan and I went back to the hotel, where he had reserved a suite for our very first night together. From what we could tell, we hadn't been followed by paparazzi. We made it inside, got into our room, and gave each other a long embrace, something we could never do in the visitors' room. We were able to doze off, only to awake to a parking lot full of news vans.

My white socks were turning brown underneath from exposure. I couldn't go the rest of the day shoeless. We had about an hour-and-a-half drive from Chillicothe to where my family was waiting for me at an Airbnb. As much as I couldn't wait to see them, I couldn't wait another minute to get something on my feet. So we made a pit stop at a shoe store, where I'd have my first interaction with media.

"Gypsy," one reporter said as Ryan and I left the shoe warehouse. "What did you buy?"

"Shoes," I said.

"Gypsy, do you have plans?"

"Lots of them," I said, while thinking, *What is this man following me for?*

While we drove, I leaned my head against the glass, watching Ryan trying to lose the paparazzi following him. We feared they'd follow us to the Airbnb.

And then Ryan's phone rang.

The conditions of my parole were a bit wonky. Usually, you are not allowed to leave the state and must regularly report to your parole officer. Since I was married to a man from Louisiana, and my entire support system was also there, we had to get special approval for me to leave Missouri. This meant that until I got to Louisiana on New Year's Day, I was under the jurisdiction of the Missouri Department of Corrections, after which I would be transferred from having a Missouri parole officer (PO) to one in Louisiana.

I was supposed to spend four days with my family at the Airbnb. People had driven from all over the country to greet me and celebrate. It was to be a bonding period and also a regrouping. Ryan and I would then go to the football game and head home to our apartment the next day.

You know what they say about making plans?

Ryan's caller ID was explicit. It was my parole officer calling. He had terrible news. The Jackson County Sheriff's Office, which oversees Kansas City, wanted "her out of the state immediately."

Wait? What? We had the whole week preapproved. We'd been planning this for months. What about the party? My family who took off from work?

"You have until three o'clock to leave."

"But it's already one!" Ryan said.

The rest of the ride was not joyful. Instead of walking triumphantly in to greet my family, on the verge of hyperventilating.

Mike Stanfield received me with open arms, my defender even now, and firmly said, "Tell me what they said."

Panic and paranoia pumped through my body. I was inconsolable. I felt trapped. Claustrophobic. I excused myself and went to a quiet place. My senses were overloaded. I had never been around this many people. I kept looking at the clock thinking I had to be somewhere. I realized my body clock was waiting for count time. All the ruckus and confusion felt like a virus.

The PO then blindsided us with more bad news. Once I left Missouri, the transfer of authority to Louisiana couldn't happen until the offices reopened on January 3. "She needs to be on lockdown in her apartment until she sees her PO in Louisiana," the PO said.

"That's seven days!" I cried.

"What about going to my mother's house for a dinner she's been planning?" Ryan asked, as if the PO was in a bargaining mood.

"Absolutely nowhere. She cannot leave the house for any reason at all, except to meet her parole officer."

In total lawyer mode, Mike dialed my PO from his phone while I waited in purgatory for others to slap down a verdict on my life. This time, I hadn't done anything wrong.

Gypsy will never be free.

I let self-pity take over. *You stupid idiot. You thought you'd just get out, be married, open presents, and eat cake? Gorge yourself on Dad's gumbo and have a sisterly sleepover with Mia? Ring in a new year, a new life? Fucking moron. Dumb. Dumb. So dumb.*

It was as if Chillicothe had let me out only to boomerang me back. Freedom was an illusion. My decisions on how to spend my holiday were not mine. A dose of humility and reality knocked me over. I was back to not speaking for myself. Other people were speaking on my behalf, referring to me as "she" and "her." *Did I even matter?* While my forty-plus guests had side conversations about what Mike was accomplishing on the phone, I was catapulted back to Volunteer Way. I was confined to a wheelchair. I was back in the closet at Daddy Claude's. In the alleyway with my mother. Tied to the bedpost. Running away and dragged back. The Airbnb was the shed. It was the scalpel that traced my throat. It was the hole.

I just wanted out. *I'm sorry. I'm so sorry. I'll be good.*

The sheriff's office explained to Mike that I posed a security risk. This made me feel shamefully aware of what people really thought of me. I was an imposter in a world that thinks I'm a monster. It was a foreshadowing of public opinion, and I was not in the least ready for it. Mike, though, worked his magic. The PO agreed to let me have until noon the next day to drive home. I didn't have to leave Missouri that instant. I could at least spend some time with those who love me, watch my dad open the present I bought him, and get a good night's sleep.

The next day it was back to lockdown.

TWENTY-TWO

Joie De Vivre

Joy of living

I'd been here before. I don't mean in a car with a husband on a thirteen-hour road trip. I'd been detained and contained before. Nothing that I had experienced in my entire life made any sense. Like my mother's abuse, the doctors' negligence, suicide watch, and the hole, the explanation for my rapid departure from Kansas City was vague: "a security risk." Getting in the car with Ryan the next morning, per our orders, I felt like an explanation mattered.

We loaded the car with the gifts we received the night before. Opening presents in front of my friends and family felt like a bridal shower, because I was being showered with ordinary things I needed to start a life—a life outside of prison: a plush lilac robe to match our lavender bathroom, a snow-white down puffer jacket, my first perfume à la Mia, "12 days of masking" for when I have a "spoil myself" day, and a set of makeup brushes. I was so used to using paintbrushes to put on makeup that having a pretty set was like the epitome of luxury.

When I opened a pair of chocolate-brown knee-high boots, I was so excited. I had to try them on right then, especially since my shoe size (size 6, by the way) was in question. "Hooker boots!" my dad called out, kidding but not kidding. As the room laughed, I said how I felt awkward about being the center of attention, especially during the holidays.

Then Kristy said unapologetically, "This Christmas is all about you, Baby Girl."

The unwrapping continued. A flat iron, bath bombs for my first bath in forever, a cookbook, a three-piece luggage set for the New York trip Ryan and I would be taking in January, and Mickey Mouse stemless wineglasses, for my first sip. I bought Ryan a new chain with a cross on it, and he stunned me with his mother's ring that she had given him years before, to give to his "future wife."

That was me. Someone's wife in a car on a road trip to *home*. I'd been thinking about home a lot ever since my parole was granted, when home became less an idea and more a tangible thing that belonged to me. The week prior to my release, I had to attend a mandatory seminar with all the other women who were also getting out on the same day. We were informed of logistics first. Anyone who didn't have someone coming to pick them up had to board a bus, which would take them to the depot. After that, they'd be on their own. It became clear to me how many of the women in the room were meeting nobody; they were the majority, from what I could tell.

We were given information about the conditions of parole, beginning with: Be sure to report to your parole officer. Mine was going to be out of state, so along with having a husband to pick me up, this also made me realize how unique and frankly "lucky" my situation was. There was talk about job search strategies, determining skills, and finding residences.

Somewhere about halfway through our road trip, I remembered these women, my fellow *released*. I wondered where they all were on day two. Looking out the window, I counted my blessings. I had a safe and clean place to go to, a family and support system beyond belief, and a purpose to occupy my days, including writing this book. I even had a therapist waiting. My future had more of a chance than that of many of the women sitting in the bus depot back in Missouri. Suddenly, an explanation for kicking me out of Kansas didn't matter. It did not matter at all.

What mattered was that God had decided I needed to go home. Now. Not next week. Every time something terrible happened or I was blindsided, disappointed, or disregarded, something good always came from it. I had to remember to trust, just trust that I was where I was supposed to be in that very moment. Maybe I wouldn't know why, but soon enough, when I was ready, I would.

That philosophy carries me through to this day, even after so much has happened since my release.

We got home in the wee hours of December 30 and crashed. I felt terrible that I couldn't share in the driving, but I did try to be an entertaining copilot, messing with my iPhone, pressing buttons and experimenting with sounds and displays.

Lounging around our new home was exactly what I needed. I toured the apartment, and it was just as Ryan had described it to me. I had coffee on the terrace. I couldn't have planned more pleasant weather. The fact that I could step outside anytime I wanted and let the mild Louisiana winter breeze through my hair made me giddy. I kept going back inside, just to step outside again—because I could!

Don't get me wrong. It was surreal. I felt like I was walking around in bizarro world, especially when I learned to do my very first video post on TikTok. It went viral, receiving a majority of supportive comments. From then on, I'd be following a technical and emotional learning curve. Turns out when it came to tech, I was a bit thickheaded. When it came to public opinion, I was a little thin-skinned.

We had no plans for New Year's Eve. My Dad and Kristy almost seemed enthusiastic that I had to forego the original plan to spend New Year's at the Chiefs-Saints game. On a brief check-in visit after I got home, Dad said, "Why don't we come over to your apartment, we'll cook, put on some music, just chill, you know? Just hang out together, just us."

Kristy stood nodding and smiling, as if a special private wish she had was being granted. Dad's baby blues glimmered, like this was the best idea ever.

It was.

God didn't want me ringing in a new year and a new life with 70,000 strangers. He wanted me back where he always intended me to be: home.

———————————

My mother had taken me out of Louisiana almost twenty years before. The explanations are vague, mere guesses. She had taken me from my father and family and replaced the void in my heart with lies and hurt. She had taken me away from my Cajun culture, far away from what made me *me*. She had taken so much from me. I had taken so much from her. But here I was, back where it all began—the Bayou.

That day, Dad and Kristy rushed through the front door carrying bags and bags of groceries. It was the kind of intrusion only close family has the right to—and I loved it. It was the beginning of my first holiday with family, and despite it being just the four of us, it started out busy and noisy, the way I always imagined a family spending time together.

We cooked, bantered, turned on the Saints game. Then we had a dance party in the kitchen. I never had so much fun. There were no black plastic bags on the windows, blocking out the dancing in the street. There were only the smells of spice, the sound of sweet laughter, and the smooth touch of my dad's hand as he asked me to dance.

In the small kitchen of my newlywed apartment, I had my first father-daughter dance. My dad and I swayed to Tim McGraw's "My Little Girl." He twirled me. He dipped me. He hugged me close. I closed my eyes and opened them again to make sure it was all real. The dream of a happy family I had while I was locked in the shed was not a dream at all, it was a premonition.

I realized then I had not been released. I had been returned.

Epilogue

A Day of Balance

June 10, 2024

Today marks the nine-year anniversary of the murder of my mother, Clauddine "Dee Dee" Blanchard. It is the first time I commemorate that solemn day outside of prison walls. This year, I remember the events of that early morning as a free woman. For each of the past eight years, on every June tenth, I experienced my grief and guilt the same way: with a wave of darkness hovering over me, a shadowy reminder that I would never again have a mother. I would try to connect with my mother, wherever she is—hopefully heaven. Usually, with my head under the blanket, hiding from the world, I prayed, I spoke to her out loud, I squeezed my eyes tight and concentrated, hoping to make a connection just one more time, so I could tell her how much I missed her and that I was sorry. Year after year, no matter how hard I tried, I never felt her presence in the way many people say they do after their loved ones pass away.

But this June tenth is different. On this June tenth, I myself am a mother to be.

I am pregnant. I have filed for divorce from Ryan Anderson, and I got back together with my first fiancé, Ken. He's moved to New Orleans full time as we gear up to welcome our baby in January 2025. When the ob-gyn's office called to schedule my first sonogram, where Ken and I would see our baby for the first time and hear the precious heartbeat, they suggested we do it on Monday, June tenth.

I do not think this is a coincidence.

Whether it's a message, a sign, or the balance of the universe (or all three), what had been a date defined by scandal and horror and sadness beyond comprehension has now become a day of excitement, joy, and celebration of life itself. With one phone call and a calendar appointment, a day of darkness has been transformed into a day of light. The shadowy wave is no longer hovering over me; I am able to ride it.

I believe God rights wrongs. I believe in balance.

Regardless of everything that my mother and I went through with each other—what I did to her and what she did to me—I'm now carrying her grandchild. Later today, when I see my baby on the doctor's monitor, I will wish that my mom was here for this. Maybe this means she is. June 10 no longer has to mark an ending, but a beginning. On future June tenths, I will continue to remember the sadness of my last moments with my mother, but now it will also be the day I experienced the miracle of my first moments with my baby.

I like to think that my mother is telling me that she wants me to move on with my life, that she forgives me. And what I will do on this anniversary is her way of helping me change the way I think of myself every June 10. Maybe now, with my freedom, we can both be released from our purgatories. Maybe now she can be free too. She always said we were two sides of the same penny.

Those words that used to haunt me, *Gypsy will never be happy. She will never be free*, have been once and for all put to rest. Nothing will ever erase the fact that I helped take life. But all the same, nothing will mar my joy at the incredible good fortune that I am now helping give life.

Balance is a beautiful force of nature.

As I write this, I am about at the halfway mark of my year of release from Chillicothe Correctional Center, perfect timing to notice how balance in my life is regulating the chaos that once was. Six months have gone by as quickly as a football season. And I can say with full confidence that despite what you might have seen or read about me, I've managed to hold on to the ball more than I've fumbled it.

In just six months, I've publicly gone from newlywed to divorcée, from Missourian to Louisianan, from brunette to blonde, from inmate to reality star, from uneducated to published author (twice!). Y'all, in the past six months, I've also managed to make a lifetime of mistakes, be called a gazillion names, and sneak in some necessary, smart decisions. I've misused social media, given too much credence to critics and haters, and have done and said things I regret. I was free for the first time, playing catch-up with technology, current events, even lingo, so like a fawn lifting herself up on wobbly legs, it took me a minute to find my footing.

Initially, even though I was no longer behind prison walls of barbed wire, I still felt a sense of being trapped by my negative image because of what I'm notorious for. It's been a constant struggle trying to break free from a title that was put on me, especially while trying to balance who I really am in a world I had never lived in, not for one day. It took six months to discover that I can't please everybody. So I stopped. It's much better to be myself than to try to conform to what everybody wants me to be.

I feel like people keep trying to put me in a box of either victim or murderer. But I'm not a hero; I'm not the villain either. I don't think that there is any villain in this story. After you learn more of my mother's backstory and read about her childhood and the molestation and abuse that she endured, you see she didn't have much of a start in life either. Life isn't black and white. It's not victim or perpetrator. My mom was both. I am both.

Balance makes us human.

I chose to write this memoir because I wanted to provide some more background to the story you thought you already knew. I wanted to take my story out of the sole hands of Hollywood and tip the scale a bit more evenly with my personal lived experience. I also wrote it as part of my legacy. And now, I will have two: my past story of being a daughter—and my future story of being a mother.

It will be a challenge to have difficult conversations with my child about what transpired before we became our own family. But shame is not a burden to me now. I know when the time comes for questions, I will give my child truthful answers, beginning with this book. There were only lies between my mother and me. Now, I only have truth to give.

To my unborn baby, when you are one day ready to read your mama's story and learn of your ancestry, I want you to know that every choice that I have made in my life, whether it be wrong or right, has been with the hope of having you.

Resources

Munchausen Support

munchausensupport.com

    This collaboration of Munchausen by proxy experts offers resources and support for therapists, family members in crisis, and survivors seeking treatment.

RAINN (Rape, Abuse & Incest National Network)

800.656.HOPE

RAINN.org

    The nation's largest anti–sexual violence organization, RAINN operates the National Sexual Assault Hotline, 800.656.HOPE, in partnership with more than 1,000 local sexual assault service providers across the country. Support, information, advice, and referrals are also available via online chat at hotline.rainn.org/online.

Acknowledgments

Gypsy-Rose

This book has been years in the making, beginning with my friend and business partner, Melissa Moore, who not only helped me articulate my story but also made me believe it could help people. Without her guidance, integrity, and friendship, I wouldn't have been able to find the vulnerability necessary to share who I am with the world.

Thank you, Melissa, for also introducing me to my coauthor Michele Matrisciani. Michele, what a ride. You taught me how to dive deeper into my story and helped me connect dots and find parallels that I wouldn't have found otherwise. Your guidance on storytelling helped me to find the courage to describe the sensitive details of my life, and your writing helped bring out the beauty in my survival with eloquence and grace.

Michele and Melissa brought with them esteemed agent Marilyn Allen, who has been so warm and encouraging as she shepherded the book through the daunting publishing process. Thank you, Marilyn, for the hours of work you put in not only to secure us a great publisher but for the logistical help as the details of my life changed so rapidly, which required your extra assistance.

To Glenn Yeffeth, CEO and publisher of BenBella Books, thank you for believing in my story when so many others ran the other way. You and your team always made me feel worthy of writing my story and not like someone who should be ashamed. I know there were so many moving parts to making this a reality, especially while I was still in prison, and I commend the flexibility and ingenuity of the entire team, in particular Heather Butterfield in marketing, Monica Lowry in production, and Rick Chillot, our very talented editor.

To my close friends and family, thank you for always cheering me on. To my sister, Mia, and brother, Dylan, thank you for agreeing to be featured in this book and for making me feel like I have always been an active part of your life.

Kristy and Dad, who acted as my memory when I needed it, you are my dream mother and father who are the embodiment of unconditional love. Thank you for reading this manuscript, being interviewed, and for your honesty, both public and private, about the journey we have all taken over the last thirty-three years of my life.

To all of you out there who have written to me, engaged positively with me on social media, and generally champion my day-to-day, thank you for being a supportive community and for reading *My Time to Stand*. I hope it inspires you to stand tall in the face of your own challenges or adversity. You deserve it.

Melissa

This book would not be possible without Gypsy-Rose Blanchard having the courage to first tell her story, and then second to trust Michele and me with it. I have so much gratitude to Gypsy for being open to looking at the most painful and pleasurable moments of the past without self-editing. Her unfiltered honesty comes through every word on these pages.

Many thanks to Michele Matrisciani for diving into hours of "Hey, it's Gypsy!" phone calls and transcripts to mine for the stories that are now within this book. Thank you for your countless hours of conducting phone calls and interviews with Gypsy and her family, for your invaluable advice, and our numerous conversations in which you helped sharpen the concept. You are a poet and a gifted storyteller who is able to draw out the private inner world of a woman's mind and intentions intuitively and, somehow, in her own voice. You are magic with a pen and PC.

Thank you to Kristy and Rod Blanchard for your assistance in obtaining medical records, photographs, and for helping with the voluminous amount of research on Gypsy's history.

Somehow we are lucky enough to have the tireless advocacy of our agent, Marilyn Allen; thank you for all your invaluable advice and for being a champion for this memoir.

I have many people to thank at our publisher, BenBella Books, most importantly our editor, Rick Chillot, for all his much appreciated work on the text, and marketing director Heather Butterfield.

To my children, Aspen and Jake Moore, your support allows me to pursue wholeheartedly the craft of storytelling in media and memoir for trauma survivors. Thank you for welcoming Gypsy into our family.

Most personally, I cannot begin to count the saving insights and raw kindnesses of my husband, Steve Kenoyer, who somehow tolerated my unpredictable work schedule and whose partnership makes everything seem possible.

Michele

First and foremost, I acknowledge all of the survivors of abuse, trauma, and addiction. My career has been one of championing stories of recovery: putting shame, regret, and healing into words for all of us to share and grow from. I am so humbled and grateful to learn from your extraordinary journeys and hard-earned wisdom. May you find continued strength.

The making of this book has been such a rewarding experience because of the people who have made each part of the process exceptional. Thank you, first and foremost, Melissa Moore, who is not only a talent beyond measure, but a woman with integrity and pure passion for helping people tell their stories. Your unwavering belief in my abilities lifts me up and inspires me with each project we do together. It's an honor being your writing partner.

To Gypsy-Rose, thank you for trusting me with what you have described as your legacy. This journey has been one of the most rewarding experiences I've had in publishing yet.

Marilyn Allen, agent and friend, you have been my cheerleader, sounding board, and constant reminder of the good old days in publishing. We are still managing to have fun, and I am forever grateful for your unwavering support and the hard work you do behind the scenes. More to come!

A big shout out to the BenBella team, with Glenn Yeffeth at the helm, for being the most enthusiastic, hands-on, efficient team I've worked with in a long time. Thank you for believing in this project and for making writing two books in six months seem easy!

A BIG thank you to our editor, Rick Chillot, you've been a blast to work with. Your taking my calls, listening to my brainstorming, and overall having the patience and ability to follow my train of thought is so appreciated. Talking shop with you has been so cool. I look forward to hopefully working again with you in the future.

Thank you, Mom. Working on so many books over the years about tragedy fills my heart with gratitude that you loved and protected me so fiercely, even now. I will forever love you.

For Poppo, in heaven. I feel your presence every time I open a blank page. I wish you were here.

To my beautiful, beautiful, beautiful boys and loves of my life, Daniel and Julian. Every day I breathe is for you. You are my gifts from God that I don't deserve. Your unbelievable patience with my absence (physical and mental) while I worked is something to behold. With every fiber of my being, I want to make you proud.

Matthew, my husband, who, when my resistance gets the best of me (every single damn morning!), says, "Be the professional and get to work." From day one, no one has been more supportive than you. You see something in me that I'll never see, and that's fine with me. As long as you remain by my side.

About the Authors

Gypsy-Rose Blanchard is an advocate, author, and speaker, who after eight and a half years was released from prison. Her unbelievable story of abuse has touched millions of people around the world and raised awareness of Munchausen syndrome by proxy, a mental health disorder in which a caregiver falsely claims that another person, typically their child, is sick, injured, or has a disease. Gypsy's abuse is one of the most significant stories of Munchausen by proxy known to the public, causing her to have been unnecessarily treated with harmful medications, surgeries, and physical and emotional abuse at the hands of her mother, Dee Dee Blanchard. Gypsy-Rose's mission is to support other children who are abused and to provide knowledge to the medical establishment that might otherwise be deceived by a person with this psychological disease.

Photo credit: Jake A. Moore

Melissa Moore is an Emmy-nominated executive producer and investigative journalist, host and special correspondent of several true crime TV programs and podcasts, advocate for families of victims and perpetrators, and author. Melissa's book *Shattered Silence: The Untold Story of a Serial Killer's Daughter* described her discovery that her father, Keith Jesperson, was the infamous "Happy Face Killer" who murdered eight women in the early 1990s.

Melissa was the true crime correspondent for *The Dr. Oz Show*'s "True-Crime Tuesdays" for four years (2016–2019), during which time she developed more than seventy episodes. Melissa created and hosted *Monster in My Family*, which ran for two seasons (2015, 2017) on Lifetime, where she was the executive producer. She was also a special correspondent for the daytime TV newsmagazine *Crime Watch Daily* and was nominated in 2016 for an Emmy Award for her investigative work.

She is the executive producer and host of several podcasts for iHeartMedia, including *Happy Face* and *Happy Face Presents: Two Face*, for which she won the Best Breakout New Podcast Award from iHeart. CBS All Access is adapting the *Happy Face* podcast for TV.

Melissa also coauthored a self-help book, *Whole: How I Learned to Fill the Fragments of My Life with Forgiveness, Hope, Strength, and Creativity* (Rodale, 2016), which was well reviewed by *Publishers Weekly* and received a starred *Booklist* review: "There is a wealth of wisdom here for anyone, whether he or she is struggling with an unhappy childhood, struggling with his or her own addiction or that of loved ones, or just trying to cope with life."

Photo credit: Lara E. Hart

Michele Matrisciani is a veteran publishing professional and a *New York Times* bestselling editor and former editorial director of HCI Books—the original publisher of *Chicken Soup for the Soul* and the harrowing blockbuster memoir of parental abuse *A Child Called "It."* Specializing in memoir and prescriptive nonfiction, Michele was an acquisitions editor and developmental editor for fifteen years. In 2011, Michele founded Bookchic LLC, a full-service content development consulting company. She is the coauthor with Melissa Moore of *Whole: How I Learned to Fill the Fragments of My Life with Forgiveness, Hope, Strength, and Creativity.*

Michele will earn her MFA in creative writing from Stony Brook University in 2024. She is a Pushcart Prize nominee for her personal essay "The Case for the Second Mom."

Visit Michele at www.michelem.net.